NEW Jewish CUISINE

NEW Jewish CUISINE

Contemporary Kosher Cooking from Around the World

by Carole Sobell

photography by Laurie Evans

Interlink Books
An imprint of Interlink Publishing Group, Inc.
New York • Northampton

I would like to give a special thank you to my Mum and Ernie for all their love, guidance, and support; to Sylvia and Harold Sobell for everything they taught me; and to my children, Bianca and Jonathan, for their patience and who mean the world to me. Another special thank you to Hilary and Cyril Dennis, Andrea, Victoria, and Jonathan for their continued family friendship and support.

Photographer: Laurie Evans
Stylist: Lesley Richardson
Photographic assistant: Andy Grimshaw
Designer: Robert Kelland
Editor: Phil McNeill

With thanks to Rachel Bentham, Juliette Ellis, Rick Fowden, Judith Hannam, Dawn Kohn, Clair Reynolds, Caroline Warde, to Jake Watkins for his outstanding culinary expertise in the line of fire, and to Lara Piercy and Rob Brown at Colour Systems. My special thanks to Scott MacRae, whose advice and patience were invaluable.

First American edition published in 2002 by

INTERLINK BOOKS

An imprint of Interlink Publishing Group, Inc., 99 Seventh Avenue, Brooklyn, New York 11215 and 46 Crosby Street, Northampton, Massachusetts 01060

www.interlinkbooks.com

Text copyright © Kuperard 2002

American edition copyright © Interlink Publishing 2002

Library of Congress Cataloging-in-Publication Data

Sobell, Carole.
  New Jewish cuisine / by Carole Sobell ; photography by Laurie Evans.— 1st American ed.
    p. cm.
  ISBN 1-56656-450-6
  1. Cookery, Jewish. 2. Cookery, International. I. Title.
  TX724 .S588 2002
  641.5'676—dc21
                              2001008159

Printed and bound in Italy by Giunti Industrie Grafiche

Contents

6

What exactly makes a dish "Jewish?" So many diverse cultures have had an influence on our food over the years that it is now truly international. Jewish communities scattered across the globe have all brought their own distinctive local elements to bear. Today, recipes that can trace their origins back to biblical times sit comfortably alongside more modern offerings.

Contemporary Jewish food is a truly cosmopolitan mix—and Carole Sobell, as a leading Jewish caterer, has taken that one step further by integrating the best of the world's cuisines into the food she presents to her guests. Now, when Sobell draws up a menu for a banquet, the only question that really matters is: "Is it kosher?"

The Hebrew word kosher literally means "fit." The religious laws of *kashrut* lay down strict rules to ensure that food is "fit" for the Jewish table. Meat must come only from animals that have a split hoof and chew the cud, which allows for cattle, sheep, and goats, for example, but excludes pigs, as well as horses and camels. To be kosher, meat or fowl must only come from ritually slaughtered animals and must be salted, soaked, or broiled to remove the blood, as it is strictly forbidden to eat it. Fish must have fins and scales—which excludes all shellfish. The Bible also contains a precise list of non-kosher fowl, which includes birds of prey.

In culinary terms, one of the most restrictive rules is the separation of milk and meat, which must not be cooked or served together in the same meal. The rule can be traced to the biblical command "You shall not boil a kid in its mother's milk," which was interpreted to mean that meat and dairy must be kept separate.

Readers from more orthodox communities will automatically recognize the practical application of this law. At home, you will use separate cooking dishes and utensils for milk and meat dishes. You may even have entirely separate milk and meat sinks, and food storage and preparation areas. Your favorite Jewish restaurants may have completely separate milk and meat kitchens, or you may prefer to choose between dairy and meat restaurants when dining out.

For a kosher catering company such as Carole Sobell's, obtaining the necessary license from the rabbinical authorities is very exacting, and non-Jews often find the restrictions bewildering. "You mean you follow all these complicated rules—and still manage to produce delicious food!" It's a bit like asking a champion boxer to fight with one hand tied behind his back, and is not the kind of thing with which your average temperamental chef has to cope.

The most notable difference, in practical terms, between a Jewish and non-Jewish caterer's kitchen is the presence of the *shomer*—a person trained in the laws of *kashrut*—who has to be on the premises during any food preparation to check and authorize each stage, from lighting the ovens to serving the food.

Koshering a kitchen that is to be used for food preparation at an outside venue takes around three hours. The ovens are "burned out" for at least an hour to rid them of any food particles, and the caterers will then install their own oven racks, or fix chicken wire to existing racks so that food does not come into contact with surfaces that may have been previously used to cook non-kosher foods.

In addition, all work surfaces are covered in foil, and dairy and meat products strategically separated.

Great care is taken to ensure the use of correct cooking utensils, which are labeled with blue tape for dairy and red for meat. A wrongly labeled utensil that has been left in

7

the kitchen during any stage of preparing either meat or dairy dishes is quickly confiscated by the *shomer*, who has the authority to stop an event going ahead at any stage if he is not satisfied that every aspect of Jewish dietary law is fully met.

Any food that is to be served must pass the watchful eye of the shomer before it leaves the kitchen. All produce is thoroughly inspected. Salad leaves and green vegetables are shaken and examined against sheets of white paper for any sign of insects, whose consumption is strictly forbidden under Jewish law.

Wine and drinks to be served at the bar must also be 100 percent kosher. For wine to be kosher, it must have a rabbinical seal of approval, which is given only to wines whose production has been supervised by that authority right from growing the grapes to bottling the finished product.

Certifying kosher wines is a complex business that has its roots in ancient Talmudic law. The law stated that it was strictly forbidden for Jews to drink wine that had been used for worshipping idols. Eventually this law encompassed all wines that had even been touched by Gentiles (non-Jews).

To many Jews, following the dietary laws is second nature, and cooks throughout the generations have experimented and adapted local recipes to suit their demands. For others, however, including those readers simply interested in adding a colorful new strand to their repertoire of recipes, these rules and restrictions may seem a little daunting.

Dinner invitations and menu planning can cause a headache for the host who is struggling to accommodate a mix of guests, some of whom keep kosher, while others do not. Add a couple of vegetarians, an allergy sufferer, and a guest requiring a low-cholesterol diet, and the only recipe facing the well-intentioned host could be one for disaster! It's worth making sure you know the dietary habits and needs of all your guests, including the question of whether they will only drink kosher wines, before you start planning your dinner party.

As for the rest of the menu, *New Jewish Cuisine* aims to simplify the matter by offering only dairy-free dishes that can therefore be served with meat or fish meals. They are also a source of inspiration for those avoiding dairy foods for health reasons alone.

This book does not seek to give an exhaustive explanation of the laws of *kashrut*, its historical origins and its application in the home. Much has already been written on the subject to satisfy those interested in learning more. What this book can do is reassure the observant that these tried and tested recipes are kosher, and where necessary have been carefully adapted to suit Jewish law while retaining their full flavors, tastes, and textures.

9

Carole Sobell's

10

Introduction • "A bit of a do..."

The act of offering hospitality is regarded as a "mitzvah," or good deed—and it is that desire to please and delight others that is the inspiration for *New Jewish Cuisine*. This book will help you entertain your guests with style, whether it's a simple snack of corned beef sandwiches or a special occasion dinner.

Drawing on over 20 years' experience in catering, Sobell has compiled a unique collection of recipes ranging from French-inspired fine dining to robust traditional rustic meals and deliciously different desserts that you will want to cook again and again. Among the collection are some favorites that have been served to the many people who turn to Sobell's successful London-based catering business for major celebrations such as weddings, bar mitzvahs, and

anniversary parties. Many of Sobell's events celebrate those "once-in-a-lifetime" moments for her clients, and their importance is reflected in the imagination and attention to detail that go into every one.

Few of us who set out to entertain are faced with the task of transporting a full-sized funfair complete with ring toss, rifle range, bumper cars, and a sawdust-strewn floor into a five-star hotel….

Sobell's dramatic creations have included a tropical jungle in a hotel ballroom, lavish marquees with star-studded ceilings, and a riverside party where each guest setting came with its own live goldfish!

Yet even the professionals have to handle those moments when something doesn't go as planned. That's

Scenes from a wedding: Sobell talking appetizers with her executive chef, Scott MacRae; with bride Lauren Rosenthal, who married Darren Tish in March 2000; and with Dorchester Hotel toastmaster David Collins, at a reception that Sobell organized.

Carole Sobell's

· Glossary ·

Agar agar Gelatin substitute, made from seaweed

Assiette An assortment

Bake blind Baking pastry on its own to form a pastry case (see page 151)

Balsamic vinegar A dark Italian vinegar with a sweet taste

Bird's-eye chili peppers Small hot red chili peppers

Blanch Boil vegetables and cool rapidly

Blowtorch Obtainable at specialty kitchen stores

Bok choy Chinese cabbage, also known as pak choi

Brisket Beef from the breast of the cow

Cape gooseberry A fruit that looks like a yellow cherry and tastes like a sweet tomato. Substitute tomatillos, gooseberries, or cherry tomatoes

Court bouillon Wine and vegetable stock used in fish dishes

Crème anglaise Custard

Crêpe A thin pancake

Croûtons Cubes of fried, roasted, or toasted bread

Crudités Raw vegetables, usually eaten with a dip

Dredger Large sugar shaker

Duck confit Duck cooked slowly in its own fat

Duxelles Sauce or stuffing made from mushrooms and shallots

Flambé Set afire by igniting spirits to remove the alcohol

Gravlax Dry-cured salmon—a dish of Scandinavian origin, also known as gravadlax

Griddle Pan with ridges for broiling on a stove to give a striped effect

Latkes Grated potato pancakes

Lockshen Jewish noodles. Vermicelli pasta is a good substitute

Mevushal Pasteurized

Nage Vegetable stock

Noisette A small, round piece of lamb or other meat

Nori Dried Japanese seaweed sheets used in sushi

Palmier A sweet pastry (originally they were shaped like palm leaves)

Pan-fry Fry in shallow oil, usually at a high temperature

Parchment paper Non-flammable paper on which food is placed for baking

Petit fours Tiny cakes or cookies, elaborately decorated

Rack of lamb The front ribs

Ramekin Small ceramic dish for baking individual portions

Reduce Boil to reduce in volume, thus thickening and/or intensifying the flavor

Rosti Grated potato, pan-fried and roasted

Skim Take the fat off the top of a stock

Sorbet Frozen mixture of water and, usually, fruit juice

Superfine sugar Also known as castor sugar, its tiny granules dissolve almost instantly. Create it at home by briefly grinding granulated sugar

Sushi A Japanese specialty consisting of a filling layered with rice, often wrapped in seaweed

Sweat Cook vegetables slowly in a little oil, bringing out their juices, with or without color

Tapenade A Provençal dip made from black olives, anchovies and capers

Tartar sauce Mayonnaise mixture with pickles and capers that usually accompanies fish

Teriyaki A sweet soy sauce

Truffle *(savory)* Strong-smelling fungus that grows underground

Truffle *(sweet)* A round chocolate-and-rum petit four

Tuile Curved cookie

Velouté Sauce made from flour, margarine, cream substitute, and stock

Wasabi Japanese horseradish

12

Almost too good to eat...Sobell adds the finishing touches to a tray of exquisitely-presented savory tartlets

when a party organizer's greatest asset is her sense of humor...Sobell laughs as she remembers one particular party when thousands of scented rose petals fell romantically from the ceiling—and promptly turned the dance floor into a dangerously slippery surface. Not wishing to interrupt the dance, out came a broom, which, as a tango partner, soon cleared the petals without disturbing anyone.

No effort is spared, whether Sobell is catering for a client's party or entertaining her own friends and family at home. A self-confessed chocolate lover, she likes nothing

better than treating her guests to a selection of amazing desserts or trays of mouth-watering appetizers, all beautifully presented—and many of her favorites are included in this book for you to create at home.

Larger, stage-managed events have to be run like a military operation with Sobell, front of house, linked by walkie-talkie radio to her key staff in the kitchens and at the tables. It may be organized bedlam behind the scenes, but she ensures that the show runs smoothly, leaving the party host and guests to have a great time. And if you stick

14

Shaken but not stirred...Sobell loves to highlight her dishes with a dusting of powdered sugar.

to the same careful planning, it should guarantee successful entertaining at home—walkie-talkies optional!

As Sobell says, it doesn't matter whether the dinner you are creating is for two or two hundred, you can make it happen, and make it memorable for all the right reasons. With a little forethought about setting the scene and presenting the food well, it need not be too difficult to make a lasting impression.

New Jewish Cuisine, with its tried-and-tested recipes presented in a modern restaurant style, is designed to help you dazzle.

Responding to the trend toward eating out more, fueled by foreign travel and a more knowledgeable and sophisticated consumer, the recipes are drawn from a wide variety of culinary styles and cultures.

Sobell's love of experimenting with new ways to

present food began in her late teens, when she would prepare the family's evening meal and hope to surprise them with what was offered. Among this collection, therefore, you will find that many classic Jewish dishes such as smoked salmon have been given a new twist, as in the Assiette of Salmon—Teriyaki, Smoked, and Gravlax—with Oriental Salad. Elsewhere, modern-day classics such as Seared Tuna with Arugula and a Lime and Ginger Dressing, and Far Eastern dishes such as Thai Chicken Curry with Basmati Rice, sit alongside classic comfort-foods such as Traditional Chicken Soup.

All the recipes are kosher and dairy-free, and allow the reader to plan and serve exciting meals for any occasion with confidence. *New Jewish Cuisine* should help you to create your own special occasions—and share in Sobell's love of "making it happen."

15

Don't forget to leave room for the plates!

Appetizers

Opposite, clockwise from top left: Filo Tartlets with Black Olives, Cherry Tomatoes, and Basil; Smoked Salmon Rosettes; Smoked Salmon and Potato Stacks; Smoked Salmon Parcels; Salmon in Filo; Smoked Salmon Rosettes

Smoked Salmon Mousse

B a s e   r e c i p e

5½ ounces smoked salmon
3 tablespoons cold vegetable stock (see page 79)
4 tablespoons mayonnaise
juice of ½ lemon
freshly ground black pepper

Blend all the ingredients until smooth, then chill.

Smoked Salmon Parcels

M a k e s   2 0   p a r c e l s

1 x Smoked Salmon Mousse recipe (see above)
20 x 2-inch squares smoked salmon
1 bunch chives, blanched in boiling salted water

Put a teaspoon of mousse in the center of each smoked salmon square. Tie a blanched chive around each square.

Smoked Salmon Roulades

M a k e s   2 0 – 2 5   r o u l a d e s

1 x Smoked Salmon Mousse recipe (see above)
4 slices smoked salmon

Lay the smoked salmon on a sheet of plastic wrap. Smooth the mousse over it and roll like a roulade. Chill for 2 hours. Slice into small discs and place on toasted croûtons (see page 37) or on thickly sliced cucumber.

Smoked Salmon Rosettes

M a k e s   2 0   r o s e t t e s

10–12 ounces smoked salmon, cut into ribbons
20 rounds toasted white, rye, or pumpernickel bread
1 bunch chives, chopped
freshly ground black pepper

Roll the salmon ribbons into flower shapes—the easiest way to do this is with a pastry cutter. Place on the bread. Garnish with the chives and season with pepper.

Salmon in Filo

M a k e s   2 0

3½ ounces cooked salmon
3½ ounces smoked salmon, diced
½ medium tomato, skinned, seeds removed, and diced
½ medium red pepper, diced
salt and freshly ground black pepper
1 bunch chives, chopped
1 package filo pastry
olive oil

Preheat the oven to 375°F.

Mix together the salmon, smoked salmon, tomato, and red pepper, and season with salt and pepper and chopped chives.

Brush two sheets of filo with olive oil then cut into 1⅓-inch squares. Place a teaspoon of the salmon mixture in the center of each square and shape into small, square packages.

On a baking sheet, place the "packages" on parchment or wax paper and bake for 4–5 minutes until golden. Serve warm.

Carole Sobell's

Gravlax with Dill Blinis

Makes 12

1 x 2¼-pound side of salmon, skin on
7½ cups flaked sea salt
1¼ cups sugar
zest and juice of a lemon
zest and juice of a lime
2 bunches dill, finely chopped
4 teaspoons mayonnaise

Mix the salt and sugar with the lemon and lime zest and juice. Line a plastic tray with plastic wrap, then cover with half the salt mixture. Lay the salmon, skin side down, on top, and sprinkle with the dill. Cover with the remaining salt mixture.

Wrap the plastic wrap tightly around the salmon, using more if necessary. Place another plastic tray on top, weight with something heavy, put in the refrigerator, and leave for 24 hours, turning the salmon every 6 hours or so.

Scrape off any remaining salt and sugar, and slice very thinly. The gravlax will keep for a week.

BLINIS—FOR THE LEAVENING
2 tablespoons yeast
1 cup lukewarm soy milk
¼ cup all-purpose flour
≈
BLINIS—FOR THE BATTER
1 cup buckwheat flour
2 eggs, separated
salt

Whisk together the leavening ingredients and leave in a warm place for 2 hours. Then mix the buckwheat flour and egg yolks into the leavening mixture and let sit for 1 hour.

Whisk the egg whites with a pinch of salt until stiff peaks form, then fold into the flour mixture.

Heat a large frying pan, brushed with a little oil, then pour a small teaspoon of batter into the center and fry each side for 90 seconds. Drain on paper towel and cool. Continue until all the batter has been used.

Spread mayonnaise lightly on the blinis and place fine slices of gravlax on top. Garnish with freshly-picked dill.

❋ Blinis can be made larger and used as a breakfast dish, under scrambled eggs, for example, as an alternative to bagels.

Smoked Salmon and Potato Stacks

Makes 20

4–5 medium potatoes, peeled and thinly sliced
1 pound 2 ounces smoked salmon
salt and freshly ground black pepper
2 cups vegetable stock (see page 79)

Preheat the oven to 375°F.

Line a greased baking pan with two layers of potatoes, season lightly, then add a layer of smoked salmon, and then a small ladle of vegetable stock. Repeat these layers until all the potatoes, salmon, and stock have been used, finishing with a layer of potato.

Cover with aluminum foil and bake for an hour until tender and cooked through. Weight with something heavy, then chill in refrigerator. To serve, cut into ¾-inch squares.

❋ To make the cutting easier, line the baking pan with lightly-greased parchment paper before starting. At the end, you can then lift the whole dish out of the tray onto a cutting board.

19

Sushi

Makes approximately 25 pieces

Sushi Rice

3½ cups short grain rice
4 cups water
≈
SUSHI VINEGAR
5 tablespoons rice vinegar
2 tablespoons sugar
pinch of salt

Wash the rice in cold water at least three times to remove the excess starch. Bring water and rice to a boil and cook for 2 minutes, uncovered. Then let it simmer, covered, for 15–20 minutes, until the water has been absorbed.

While the rice is cooking, combine the vinegar, sugar, and salt in a bowl. Mix thoroughly so all sugar and salt dissolve.

Remove from the heat, take off the lid, and let stand for 5 minutes, then fold the sugar and salt solution into the cooked rice. Cover with a clean dish towel and allow to stand for another 5 minutes. The rice is now ready to use.

Temaki Sushi

Temaki is cone-shaped. Using the same ingredients as above right for Maki Sushi, place a triangular half-sheet of nori with one corner facing you, one facing away, and one to the left. Place a little rice and wasabi by the left corner. Bring the far corner toward you, overlapping the near corner to make a cone, leaving a little of the filling you choose showing.

Maki Sushi (Sushi Rolls)

nori (dried Japanese seaweed sheets)
bowl of vinegared water
prepared rice
wasabi (Japanese horseradish)
fillings as below
≈
FILLINGS (1½-INCHES LONG X ¼-INCH SQUARED)
raw salmon strips
raw tuna strips (remove dark meat)
cucumber strips (without seeds)
carrot strips (boiled in hot water for 3 minutes, then refresh in cold water until cold)

The traditional way of creating maki sushi is to do it on a small bamboo mat. Place a sheet of nori, shiny side down, on the mat. Wet your right hand in the vinegared water, take a ball of rice and spread it with your moistened hand in an even layer over half of the nori. Create a shallow groove along the middle of the rice bed. Smear wasabi in this groove. Arrange the strips and pieces of vegetables and fish on top of the wasabi.

Lift the end of the mat, and use your thumbs to tuck the nearest edge of nori against the rice, then gently roll the mat away from you, pressing the ingredients together. The nori sheet edges should overlap to seal the completed roll.

Slice the rolls gently with a very sharp knife. Serve as soon as possible, so that the seaweed is still a bit crispy.

Opposite: Maki Sushi

Filo Tartlets with Broiled Salmon, Ginger, and Avocado

Makes 20

This colorful special-occasion appetizer looks so appealing when presented as an individual tartlet garnished with summer leaves. Bags of mixed salad leaves are, of course, readily available in supermarkets and are perfect for adding the finishing touch to the plate.

1 package filo pastry
1 pound 2 ounces salmon, sliced
2-inch piece fresh root ginger, finely grated
3 tablespoons olive oil
1 avocado, diced
½ medium tomato, skinned, seeds removed, and finely diced
½ medium yellow pepper, seeds removed, and finely diced
½ bunch cilantro, chopped
½ bunch basil, chopped
½ bunch dill for garnish

Preheat the oven to 425°F.

Heat a griddle pan. Lightly brush the salmon with oil. Grill it for a minute or so each side, then flake, and allow to cool. (If you haven't got a griddle pan, you can broil under a hot broiler.)

Gently cook the ginger in a little of the olive oil until colored, taking care not to burn it.

Mix the cooked salmon with the diced vegetables,

✳ Chef's Tip

Fold the salmon and avocado very carefully to keep its shape, and add the dressing at the last minute so that it does not seep into the pastry and make it soggy.

chopped herbs, ginger, and 2 tablespoons olive oil. Brush the filo with the olive oil and cut into twenty 1⅓-inch rounds. Push into small tartlet or mini muffin tins and bake for 6–8 minutes until golden.

To serve cold, fill the tartlets with the salmon mixture and add a garnish of dill.

To serve warm, gently heat the salmon mixture in a pan. Fill the tartlets and garnish with sprigs of dill.

Filo Tartlets with Black Olives, Cherry Tomatoes, and Basil

Makes 20

1 package filo pastry
2½ cups cherry tomatoes, skinned, seeds removed, and diced
⅔ cup pitted black olives, cut into quarters
2 bunches basil, finely chopped
4 tablespoons virgin olive oil
freshly ground black pepper

Make the tartlets according to the previous recipe.

Mix together the tomatoes, olives, basil, and olive oil, then leave to chill for 6 hours. Spoon into the tartlets, and serve immediately.

✳ It is essential to use good olives and ripe cherry tomatoes.

Vegetable Tempura

Serves 20

20 asparagus tips
20 broccoli florets
20 wild mushrooms, washed carefully
20 red pepper julienne strips
20 sweet potato julienne strips
1⅔ cup tempura flour
3½ cups very cold carbonated water
vegetable oil for frying
pinch of chili powder
salt and pepper

Mix together the flour and water to form a batter with the consistency of light cream. Mix in the chili powder, salt, and pepper.

Dip the vegetables in the batter, then deep-fry in oil heated to 425°F for between 45 seconds and a minute, until very crisp.

Serve hot with Sweet Chili Dipping Sauce (see page 84) or soy sauce.

Root Vegetable Crisps

Using a vegetable peeler, simply peel slices of any root vegetable you like—such as parsnips, carrots, sweet potatoes, beets—and deep-fry in oil heated to 325°F until the fryer has stopped bubbling and the vegetables are golden and crisp.

❉ Can be kept in an airtight container for up to 1 week.

Bruschetta of Roasted Peppers, Anchovies, and Capers

Serves 20

8 red peppers
40 fresh anchovy fillets
½ cup olive oil
¼ cup capers, drained and finely chopped
½ bunch basil, finely chopped
½ bunch cilantro, finely chopped
1 loaf ciabatta bread (cut into ½-inch rounds)

Preheat the oven to 500°F, then roast the peppers for 10 minutes until the skins are blackened. Place in a plastic bag and close tightly (or use a bowl sealed with plastic wrap). When cool enough to handle, skin, remove seeds, and cut into diamonds.

Using cocktail sticks, skewer the anchovies and red pepper, two pieces of each per stick.

Warm the olive oil, add the capers and herbs, brush generously over the sliced ciabatta and toast under the broiler.

Place skewered anchovies and peppers on ciabatta bread and serve immediately.

23

Thai Chicken Satay

Makes 50

The distinctive flavors of lemongrass, lime leaves, and chili peppers conjure up a taste of Asia on neat, easy-to-handle skewers, which make satay an ideal appetizer for entertaining. Thai cuisine is an increasingly popular choice for home entertaining, and Thai herbs and spices are now readily available in major supermarkets.

6 chicken breasts, cut into thin strips
6–8 chili peppers, chopped
10–12 cloves garlic, chopped
2 x 3-inch pieces lemongrass, chopped
1 bunch cilantro
1 bunch basil
4 lime leaves
4 cups peanuts
¾ cup sesame oil
1 cup coconut milk

Place all the ingredients, except for the chicken, in a food processor and blend to a fine paste.

Take half the satay marinade and simmer over low heat for 20 minutes. Allow to cool. This will be used as a dip.

Meanwhile, brush the rest of the marinade over the chicken pieces, then skewer them onto wooden skewers that have been previously soaked in water to prevent the wood burning. Cook under a medium-hot broiler for 4 minutes each side or until the chicken is cooked through. Serve warm, with the satay dip.

❋ Chef's Tip

Leave the chicken pieces to soak up the flavors of the marinade for a while before cooking. For a more intense flavor they can be grilled— but it is messy!

Spring Rolls with Sweet Chili Dipping Sauce

Makes 50–60

1 package spring roll wrappers (or use filo pastry)
1 egg white
1 tablespoon sesame oil
1–2 medium leeks, cut into julienne strips
1–2 medium carrots, cut into julienne strips
2¾ cups bean sprouts
1 chili pepper, chopped
1-inch piece ginger, grated
½ bunch cilantro, chopped
2¼ teaspoons sesame seeds
vegetable oil for frying
1 x Sweet Chili Dipping Sauce recipe (see page 84)

Cut the pastry into 1½-inch squares and brush with egg white. (If you are using filo pastry, brush with sesame oil.)

Mix together the rest of the ingredients, season with sesame oil, and place a teaspoonful of the mixture in the center of each pastry square. Roll up, making sure you tuck in the ends.

Deep-fry in oil heated to 350°F until golden. Drain well on paper towels and serve with Sweet Chili Dipping Sauce.

❋ For a less fattening style, cook in a hot oven (425°F) until brown.

25

Opposite, clockwise from bottom left:
Thai Chicken Satay, Spring Rolls with Sweet
Chili Dipping Sauce, Thai Fish Cakes

Goujons of Sole with Tartar Sauce

Serves 20

1 pound 11 ounces lemon sole fillet
¾ cup seasoned flour
3 eggs, beaten
2 cups white breadcrumbs
vegetable oil
1 x Tartar Sauce recipe (see page 83)

Cut the lemon sole into julienne strips about the size of your little finger. Dip first in the seasoned flour, then in the egg, and then roll in the breadcrumbs. Chill in refrigerator for at least 15 minutes. (May be stored in freezer.)

Fry these goujons in very hot oil for 2 minutes until crisp and golden. Drain well on paper towel, season with salt, and serve with Tartar Sauce and a wedge of lemon.

French Fries

Serves 20

4 large baking potatoes, peeled
oil for frying
salt

Slice the potatoes finely and then cut into julienne strips. Rinse in cold water and drain well. Deep-fry at 350°F for 2 minutes until golden brown. Drain on paper towel. Season with salt.

Fish and Chips

Serves 20

1 x Goujons of Sole recipe
1 x French Fries recipe
1 x Tartar Sauce recipe (see page 83)

Prepare Goujons of Sole and French Fries, see recipes at left, and serve in paper cones with Tartar Sauce and lemon wedges to accompany.

Herb Sausages with Honey and Sesame Seeds

Makes 20

20 small herb sausages
½ cup honey
1 tablespoon soy sauce
⅓ cup black-and-white sesame seeds
⅜ cup sesame oil

Broil or bake the sausages until golden. Mix the honey, soy sauce, sesame seeds, and sesame oil together in an ovenproof bowl, and place in a hot oven for 30 seconds.

Just before serving, pour the honey and sesame seed mixture over the sausages. Serve warm.

✣ A good-quality herb mustard goes well as a dip.

Opposite: Fish and Chips

26

28

Duck in Pancakes

Makes 20 pancakes

2 x large 3-pound ducks
⅓ cup honey
1-inch piece fresh root ginger
3 tablespoons whole coriander seeds
1 cup pineapple juice
1½ tablespoons rice vinegar
3 tablespoons soy sauce
1 bunch scallions, cut into julienne strips
1 large cucumber, peeled and cut into julienne strips
20 Chinese pancakes
Hoisin sauce, to accompany

Preheat the oven to 225°F, then roast the ducks for 6 hours in a deep roasting pan on a wire rack. When handling, be careful of the hot fat which will run into the pan.

Place the honey, ginger, coriander seeds, pineapple juice, rice vinegar, and soy sauce in a pan, bring to a boil, and simmer for 5 minutes.

Take the ducks out of the oven and drain the fat from the pan. The fat can be kept in the refrigerator and used in other recipes such as Confit of Duck (see page 104).

Pour half of the honey and ginger sauce over the ducks.

Increase oven temperature to 450°F. Roast for a further 20–25 minutes until the ducks are golden and crispy.

Allow the ducks to cool, then shred the meat, mix with the scallions and cucumber and the rest of the sauce, and wrap in warmed Chinese pancakes. Serve with Hoisin sauce.

✣ The traditional Chinese way to serve this dish is to put all the ingredients separately on the table and let guests help themselves.

Opposite: Duck in Pancakes

Thai Fish Cakes

Makes 40 fish cakes

The modern gefilte fish ball! A very popular dish and a good alternative if you want to break from tradition and offer your guests something a little different. These spicy fish cakes also work well as part of an Asian themed appetizer selection with other dishes such as sushi, spring rolls, and Thai chicken satay. Scrumptious and very trendy.

1 x 2¼ pound white fish fillet (such as cod or haddock)
1 cup dried breadcrumbs
½ cup ground almonds
½ cup chopped basil, mint, and cilantro
½ chili pepper, chopped
1–2 cloves garlic, chopped
½-inch piece ginger, chopped
1-inch piece lemongrass, chopped
1 tablespoon lime leaves, chopped
1½ tablespoons lemon juice
¼ cup light soy sauce
salt and pepper

29

Dice the fish in a food processor, then mix with the rest of the ingredients, cover, and leave overnight in the fridge.

Mold into small patties and fry in oil or margarine until golden brown on each side and cooked through.

Serve with Sweet Chili Dipping Sauce (see page 84).

✣ A little coconut milk can be used to sweeten the mixture.

✣ Chef's Tip
Best served warm rather than hot
to appreciate the intense mix of flavors.

Breaded Chicken Goujons

Makes 30–40

4 chicken breasts

Follow the method given for Goujons of Sole (see page 26), replacing the fish with strips of chicken breast. Serve with French Fries (see page 26) in paper cones.

❊ You can always vary the recipe by adding different combinations of herbs, poppy seeds, sesame seeds, chopped parsley, etc., to the breadcrumb mix.

Carpaccio of Beef with Lemon and Olive Oil

Serves 20
(or 4 as a first course)

1 pound 2 ounces beef fillet (trimmed rib eye)
½ cup olive oil
zest and juice of 2 lemons
course sea salt and freshly ground black pepper
bread for toasting

Ask your butcher to trim the beef and slice it paper thin. Marinate it in the olive oil and lemon zest and juice for 2 hours.

Just before to serving, season the beef with coarse sea salt, black pepper, and lemon juice.

Serve on toasted bread.

Mini Burgers in a Bun

Makes 20

1 pound 2 ounces ground beef
1 shallot, chopped
3 tablespoons fresh thyme and rosemary, chopped
1–2 cloves garlic, chopped
1 egg, beaten
½ cup dried breadcrumbs
salt and freshly ground black pepper
a squeeze of lemon juice
20 mini burger buns

Mix together the ground beef, shallots, herbs, garlic, egg, and breadcrumbs, season with salt and pepper to taste, and add a squeeze of lemon juice.

Shape into 20 mini burgers.

Either fry or grill until cooked through, about 5–6 minutes.

Serve the burgers in mini burger buns accompanied by French Fries (see page 26), pickle, and a drizzle of ketchup and/or mustard.

Mini Hot Dogs with Fried Onions

Makes 20

20 mini hot dogs
2 large onions, thinly sliced
oil or margarine for frying
20 mini finger rolls

Heat the hot dogs according to the package instructions.

Just before serving, fry the onions in a little oil or margarine until golden.

Place the hot dogs in the buns and top with the onions. Serve with Spicy Tomato Sauce (see page 81).

Crudités with a Garlic and Dill Mayonnaise

Serves 6

20 baby carrots
20 asparagus tips
20 broccoli florets
20 radishes
20 red pepper julienne strips
20 baby sweetcorn
20 cherry tomatoes
20 celery sticks, peeled
1 x Garlic and Dill Mayonnaise recipe (see page 84)

Trim all the vegetables to a uniform size. Lightly blanch the asparagus tips and the broccoli, and cool them in iced water. Serve with Garlic and Dill Mayonnaise.

Mini Potato Latkes

Makes 32 latkes

4 potatoes, peeled
1 medium onion
2 eggs
1 cup all-purpose flour
salt and freshly ground black pepper

Cut the potatoes and onions into small pieces. Drain in a colander. Add eggs, salt and pepper, then flour. Drain again in a colander.

Preheat the deep fryer to 315°F. Once the oil has reached that temperature, place an oval-shaped teaspoonful of the mixture into the hot oil and allow to cook until light brown, making sure the inside is thoroughly cooked. Remove from oil and drain.

To serve, heat the oil up to 350°F and fry the half-cooked latkes for approximately 1 minute more. Remove from oil, sprinkle with salt to taste, and serve.

31

Soups and Starters

Opposite: Teriyaki Salmon Wrapped in Filo

Traditional Chicken Soup

Serves 4 – 6

Everyone's mother makes the best chicken soup, and when you're feeling a little under the weather there's nothing better than a warm and comforting bowl of this great classic. Passed down from generation to generation, it has never been beaten and never bettered—it is, after all, the Jewish penicillin!

1 whole or half chicken or fowl with the wings and giblets
2 teaspoons salt
pinch of white pepper
1 large onion, peeled and halved
2 large carrots, peeled and halved
2 stalks celery, leaves and top 2 inches only
1 sprig of parsley
any soft eggs from inside the fowl (if used)
3 ounces vermicelli pasta

≈

FOR THE DUMPLINGS
1 package matzhah ball mix

Put the bird, wings and giblets in a large, heavy soup pot with 7½ cups water, add the salt and pepper, cover and bring to a boil, skimming off any froth with a large, wet metal spoon.

Add the onion, carrots, celery, parsley, and eggs, if using. Bring back to a boil, then reduce the heat so that the liquid is barely bubbling. Cover and continue to simmer for a further 3 hours or so, either on top of the stove or in a slow oven at 300°F, until the chicken leg feels very tender when prodded with a fork.

Strain the soup into a large bowl, reserving the carrots in a separate container. Cover the soup and place it in the refrigerator overnight.

Next day, remove any congealed fat and return the soup to the pot. (If there is a thick layer of fat, it can be heated in a separate pan to drive off any liquid and then, when it has stopped bubbling, cooled, and stored like rendered raw fat.)

Dice the carrots, and add them to the pot. Finally, add approximately one serving per person of pasta cooked in boiling water according to the package directions.

Make the dumplings according to package instructions.

Add the dumplings and reheat the soup slowly before serving.

❊ The soup will keep for three days in the refrigerator or for up to three months in the freezer.

❊ Chef's Tip

Note that this traditional recipe requires you to make the soup the day before you serve it. But, if you want to cut corners, you can leave that bit out!

Opposite: Traditional Chicken Soup

34

35

Tomato Soup with Fresh Basil

Serves 4 – 6

A beautiful, light and versatile soup that is equally suitable served before fish, chicken, or meat dishes. Choose a good, flavorsome tomato such as plum or one of the vine-ripened varieties. Roasting the tomatoes concentrates the flavors even further, and with the addition of fresh basil the soup takes on the wonderful tastes of summer.

16 medium tomatoes
6 cloves garlic
12 large shallots, peeled
⅝ cup olive oil
1 cup vegetable stock (see page 79)
2 tablespoons tomato paste
2 large bunches basil, leaves and stalks separated
salt and freshly ground black pepper

Preheat the oven to 500°F.

Place the tomatoes in a large roasting pan with the garlic and shallots, pour over the olive oil, season with a good pinch of salt, and roast for 25 minutes until the edges of the tomatoes begin to blacken.

Remove the tomato stalks and discard.

Put the tomatoes, garlic, shallots, and the juice into a large pot with the vegetable stock, add the basil stalks and tomato paste, and simmer for 20 minutes. Allow to

✳ Style Tip

Serve the soup in deep round bowls, which have been warmed in the oven, place the bowls on a plate garnished with garden leaves, and add thick crusty bread.

✳ Chef's Tip

Add chopped fresh basil at the last minute to retain the full flavor of the herb.

cool slightly, then purée and pass through a fine sieve. Return to pot, adjust consistency, and season to taste. Cornstarch mixed with a little cold water can be added to thicken the liquid.

Just before serving, garnish with shredded basil leaves and drizzle with a little olive oil.

Wild Mushroom Soup

Serves 8 – 10

2 cloves garlic, finely chopped
6 shallots, finely chopped
3 tablespoons margarine
3½ cups wild mushrooms, wiped clean and roughly chopped
3½ cups brown chicken stock (see page 80)
1 tablespoon cornstarch
1 bunch chives, finely chopped

In a saucepan with a lid, gently sweat the garlic and shallots in the margarine over a low heat until soft but not colored.

Add the mushrooms and cook slowly for 8 minutes.

Add the stock and simmer for 5 minutes.

Mix the cornstarch with a little cold water, add to the soup and cook for a further 5 minutes.

Purée and pass through a sieve. Return to the heat and adjust seasoning and consistency.

Just before serving, sprinkle with the chives.

Cream of Vegetable Soup with Garlic Croûtons

Serves 10

1 small leek, sliced
1 medium onion, cut into ½-inch pieces
2 cloves garlic, chopped
3½ tablespoons margarine
3 tablespoons olive oil
1 carrot, cut into ½-inch pieces
1 stalk celery, cut into ½-inch pieces
⅓ small celeriac, cut into ½-inch pieces
1–2 small potatoes, cut into ½-inch pieces
3½ cups vegetable stock (see page 79)
1½ teaspoons salt
1 bunch parsley, finely chopped

≈

FOR THE GARLIC CROÛTONS
8 cloves garlic
1 baguette
⅞ cup olive oil

Preheat the oven to 325°F.

Sweat the leek, onion, and garlic in the margarine and olive oil in a large pan with a lid for 5 minutes on a moderate heat.

Add the remaining vegetables, stock and salt and simmer, with the lid on, for 45 minutes. Allow to cool slightly, purée and pass through a sieve. Add salt and pepper to taste.

To make garlic croûtons: Cut the baguette into ½-inch cubes, and, in a bowl, mix together with the whole garlic cloves, olive oil, and a big pinch of course salt. Place the croûtons and garlic on a baking sheet and bake in the oven for 30 minutes or until crunchy and golden.

Adjust the seasoning of the soup to taste, reheat, then serve with the garlic croûtons and parsley.

Pumpkin Soup with Truffle Oil

Serves 4

1 leek, sliced
1 onion, chopped
oil or margarine for frying
1 large pumpkin, skinned, seeds removed, and diced
2 cups vegetable stock (see page 79)
salt and freshly ground black pepper
truffle oil

In a lidded saucepan, cook the leek and onion in a little oil or margarine until soft, but not colored. Add the pumpkin and cook for about 5 minutes until tender.

Add half the stock, season with salt and pepper, bring to a boil, then simmer for 10 minutes.

Allow the soup to cool slightly, then purée and pass through a sieve.

Adjust the seasoning and texture to taste, adding more stock if you prefer a thinner soup.

Serve very hot with a drizzle of truffle oil.

Pea and Mint Soup

Serves 6

1 onion, chopped
oil or margarine for frying
3 medium potatoes, peeled and diced
3½ cups vegetable stock (see page 79)
3 cups fresh peas, shelled
1 bunch of mint, leaves and stalks separated
salt and freshly ground black pepper

Heat a little oil or margarine in a large pot with a lid and sweat the onion until soft. Add the diced potato and cook slowly for 5 minutes, stirring to prevent sticking.

Pour in the stock, add the peas and the mint stalks, season with salt and pepper, then bring to a boil and simmer for 10 minutes.

Allow the soup to cool slightly, then purée and pass through a fine sieve.

Adjust the seasoning and texture to taste, adding more vegetable stock if you prefer a thinner soup.

Finely chop the mint leaves, stir into the soup, and serve immediately.

Borscht

Serves 6

2 onions
2 stalks celery, thinly sliced
¼ white cabbage
5 cups chicken stock
6 small beets, raw, finely diced
juice of 1 lemon
3 boiled potatoes, finely diced
1¼ cups soy milk
sugar to taste
salt and freshly ground black pepper

Sweat the onions, celery, and cabbage in the oil for five minutes, taking care not to let them brown.

Add the stock, bring to a boil, and simmer for 45 minutes. Strain through a fine sieve, return the liquid to the pot, and bring back to a boil.

Add the finely-diced beets and lemon juice. Cook for a further 45 minutes.

Remove from the heat. When slightly cooled, add the finely diced potatoes, milk, and sugar.

Heat slowly to serving temperature, add salt and pepper to taste, and serve.

�֎ The borscht can be puréed for a smooth texture, as in the opposite photograph. My mother always serves the potatoes chunky.

Opposite: Pumpkin Soup (left),
Pea and Mint Soup (center), Borscht (right)

38

39

Bean and Barley Soup

Serves 10–12

¼ cup dried white haricot beans,
          or ⅞ cup canned, drained
1 medium carrot
1 medium parsnip
1 medium rutabaga
1 medium onion
½ cup olive oil
⅓ cup pearl barley
2 cloves garlic, chopped
3½ cups brown chicken stock (see page 80)
10 sage leaves, chopped
1 sprig tarragon, chopped
2 sprigs parsley, chopped

If using dried beans, soak them overnight.

Peel and dice the carrot, parsnip, rutabaga, and onion the same size as the haricot beans.

Heat the olive oil in a heavy-bottomed, lidded saucepan, add the vegetables and garlic, and color gently for 5 minutes, stirring occasionally.

Add the stock and haricot beans, and simmer gently, with the lid on, for 45 minutes, skimming occasionally. Add the pearl barley and cook for a further 45 minutes until barley and beans are cooked. If, after this time, the beans are still hard, cook for a further 15 minutes or so.

Just before serving, add the herbs.

Roast Parsnip and Apple Soup

Serves 4

½ cup vegetable oil
2 medium parsnips, diced
2 medium apples, peeled and diced
1 medium onion, diced
2 cloves garlic, chopped
5 cups chicken stock (see page 80)
quarter of a bunch of rosemary
salt and freshly ground pepper

In a large heavy-bottomed pot, heat the vegetable oil until very hot. Add the parsnips, apples, onion, rosemary, and garlic, and brown carefully, without burning, for 5–10 minutes.

When the vegetables are nicely browned and starting to break down, add the stock. Season, bring to a boil, and simmer for 30 minutes until the vegetables are very soft.

Allow to cool slightly, then purée, pass through a sieve, and return to a clean pot. Adjust the seasoning and consistency according to taste, reheat, and serve.

❋ Chef's Tip

Season soups with salt and pepper just before serving. With creamy or fish soups use a little lemon juice to help bring out the flavors.

40

Minestrone

Serves 6

4 tablespoons olive oil
1 small or ½ medium onion, diced
2 cloves garlic, finely chopped
3⅜ cups brown chicken stock (see page 80)
1 small carrot, diced
¼ cup fresh peas, shelled
1 small potato, diced the size of the peas
1¾ ounces dried spaghetti, broken into
      1¾-inch pieces
¼ cup fresh fava beans, peeled and shelled
2 small tomatoes, skinned, seeds removed, and
      diced the size of the peas
1 bunch chives, finely chopped

Heat the olive oil in a large lidded pot and cook the carrot, onion, and garlic until soft but not colored.

Add the stock and simmer for 5 minutes.

Add the peas, potatoes, and spaghetti and simmer for a further 10 minutes.

Add the fava beans and tomatoes and simmer for another 5 minutes.

Just before serving, add the chives.

✻ May be served with garlic croûtons—see page 37.

Trio of Soups

Serves 6

12 large shallots, finely sliced
6 cloves garlic, finely sliced
⅜ cup olive oil
9 green peppers, seeds removed and finely sliced
9 red peppers, seeds removed and finely sliced
9 yellow peppers, seeds removed and finely sliced
3½ cups vegetable stock (see page 79)

Divide the shallots and garlic between three lidded pots and cook gently in the olive oil until soft but not browned.

Add the green pepper to the first of the pots, the red to the second, and the yellow to the last, and cook gently for 5 minutes.

Add a third of the vegetable stock to each of the pots, season, and simmer for a further 5 minutes.

Allow to cool slightly, purée each of the soups separately, washing the puréer in between, then return to three separate clean pots.

Adjust the seasoning to taste, and add a little more stock if necessary, so they each have a similar texture.

Reheat to boiling point. Pour into warm soup bowls—three soups in each bowl—so they have a swirled effect.

41

✻ Style Tip

To swirl the trio of soups together properly,
you really need two people! The first person
holds two pots of soup, the second holds one pot
of soup and a cocktail stick. Pour all three soups
into each soup bowl at once, while stirring
them together in the bowl with the cocktail stick.

Carole Sobell's

Ribbons of Smoked Salmon with Roasted Vegetables

Serves 4

7 ounces smoked salmon, cut into ribbons
4 baby fennel
½ cup olive oil
4 baby Belgian endives, cut in half lengthways
4 baby eggplants, cut in half lengthways
4 baby zucchini, cut in half lengthways
10 cherry tomatoes
salt and freshly ground black pepper
3 tablespoons balsamic vinegar

Preheat the oven to 500°F.

Cook the fennel for 10 minutes in boiling salted water. Drain and dry thoroughly.

Heat a large roasting pan, then put in the olive oil. Add the vegetables, a good pinch of salt and some pepper, and roast for 10 minutes.

Add the vinegar and roast for a further 10 minutes.

Remove the vegetables from the oven and place in a plastic lidded container, along with all the juices. Leave to marinate overnight.

Divide the vegetables between four small bowls, top with the smoked salmon ribbons, and serve.

❄ For a final flourish, drizzle with balsamic vinaigrette.

Crown of Melon with a Cascade of Berry Fruits

Serves 4

2 ripe melons (such as Galia, honeydew, or cantaloupe)
¾ cup raspberries
1½ cups strawberries
½ cup red currants
1 cup blueberries
¼ cup fresh mint leaves, chopped

Cut each melon in half in a zigzag style, and scoop out the seeds.

Wash and trim the soft fruit, then hull and halve the strawberries.

Spoon the soft fruit on top of each melon half. Sprinkle the chopped mint leaves over the fruits.

Opposite: Crown of Melon with a
Cascade of Berry Fruits

42

Teriyaki Salmon

Serves 4

4 x 3½-ounce salmon portions
1 cup teriyaki sauce
4 wooden kebab skewers
1 leek, thinly sliced
1 zucchini, cut into julienne strips
⅔ cup bean sprouts
1 red pepper, seeds removed and thinly sliced
1 x Sesame and Chili Dressing recipe (see page 84)

Cut each of the four salmon portions into about nine equal slices, and push onto wooden kebab skewers that have previously been soaked in water. Place in the teriyaki marinade and leave overnight.

Broil the salmon kebabs under a preheated broiler for 3 minutes, until the skin is just crisp.

Stir-fry the vegetables with a little of the teriyaki marinade and Sesame and Chili Dressing for 1 minute.

Spoon the stir-fried vegetables onto individual plates, and place a salmon kebab on top. Serve with the remaining Sesame and Chili Dressing on the side.

Teriyaki Salmon Wrapped in Filo

Serves 4

4 x 3½-ounce salmon portions, thinly sliced
1 cup teriyaki sauce
1 leek, cut into julienne strips
1 zucchini, cut into julienne strips
1 large carrot, cut into julienne strips
8 sheets filo pastry
⅔ cup bean sprouts
3 tablespoons sesame oil
3 tablespoons chili pepper sauce
3 tablespoons cilantro pesto (see page 82)

Marinate the salmon overnight in the refrigerator in ½ cup of the teriyaki sauce.

Preheat the oven to 450°F.

Heat a wok or large frying pan and stir-fry the leek, zucchini, carrot, and bean sprouts with ¼ cup of the teriyaki sauce. Allow to cool.

Brush two large pieces of filo with sesame oil. Place a tablespoon of the stir-fried vegetables on the pastry, cover with the slices of salmon, and fold the filo around and over to make a parcel.

Bake for 8 minutes, or until golden brown.

Meanwhile, warm the remaining vegetables, then spoon them onto the middle of a warm plate. Place the filo parcel on top, and drizzle the chili sauce, pesto, and remaining teriyaki sauce around it to garnish.

❋ *See picture on page 32*

45

Opposite: Teriyaki Salmon

46

Broiled Salmon and Baby Leek Terrine with Saffron and Chive Dressing

Serves 8—10

8 bunches of baby leeks
6¾ cups vegetable stock (see page 79)
2 very large leeks, cut in half lengthways
1¾ pounds salmon fillets
2 packages agar agar
pinch of saffron
1 x Saffron and Chive Dressing recipe (see page 84)
½ cup olive oil
1 medium yellow pepper, diced, to garnish

Take a 9½ x 4-inch terrine mold and line it with plastic wrap.

Simmer the baby leeks for 8 minutes in 4¼ cups of the stock. Using a slotted spoon, remove leeks from the stock, then allow to cool. Add the large leeks to the stock and blanch for 1 minute. Drain, allow to cool, dry with a cloth, then cut into ribbons.

Slice the salmon fillet into 3 thin slices of equal length, about ¼ inch thick (or ask your fishmonger to do this).

Preheat a broiler pan until very hot, brush the salmon with the olive oil, then broil on one side only, for 2 minutes or so, taking care not to overcook the fish. Leave to cool.

Warm the remaining vegetable stock and add the agar agar and saffron. Allow to cool slightly.

Lay some of the large leeks in the bottom of the terrine, put a layer of salmon on top, drizzle over some of the warm vegetable stock, then add a layer of the baby leeks. Repeat these layers until you reach the top of the mold, finishing with a layer of the large leeks.

Cover with plastic wrap, put a weight such as a small chopping board on top of the terrine, and leave in the refrigerator overnight.

Lift the terrine from the mold, using the plastic wrap to help you. With a hot knife, cut a slice and serve with the chopped pepper and the chive dressing drizzled around it.

Broiled Asparagus

Serves 6

3 large bunches of asparagus
½ cup olive oil

Preheat the broiler until very hot.

Trim the ends of the asparagus, and peel if hard or woody. Dip the asparagus in the olive oil, making sure they are well coated, then place under the broiler until lightly blackened. Serve either warm or cold.

Opposite: Chargrilled Asparagus

47

Tower of Roasted Vegetables

Serves 4

Presentation is the key to this colorful combination of roasted vegetables, which should be succulent but still have some bite. Serve on attractive large plates and stack high to feed the eyes first.

1 eggplant, sliced into ½-inch rounds
2 zucchini, sliced into ½-inch rounds
1 sprig thyme
1 sprig rosemary
2 cloves garlic, crushed
½ cup olive oil
4 red peppers
2 onions, peeled and sliced into ½-inch rings
1 x Pesto recipe (see page 82)
1 x Spicy Tomato Sauce recipe (see page 81)

Marinate the eggplant and zucchini in a mixture of the thyme, rosemary, garlic, and olive oil and let sit for a minimum of 2 hours.

Meanwhile, roast the peppers in an oven preheated to 500°F for 10 minutes. When cool enough to handle, remove the blackened skins and seeds, and cut into discs.

Heat a stove-top griddle pan or preheat a broiler. Remove the eggplant and zucchini slices from the marinade (setting this aside until later) and broil them together with the onion and the roasted peppers.

Place the broiled vegetables in an ovenproof dish, cover with the reserved marinade, and bake uncovered in an oven preheated to 325°F for 20 minutes.

On each of the four serving plates, layer the vegetables on top of each other to form a tower. Garnish each plate with drizzles of pesto and tomato sauce. Serve warm.

✳ Style Tip

Dust the serving plates
with a sprinkling of paprika
through a sieve to add
a perfect finishing touch.

Opposite: Tower of Roasted Vegetables

Carole Sobell's

Mosaic of Provençal Vegetables with Pesto

Serves 12

Imagine a long, lazy summer Sunday lunch, relaxing with great friends and good wine and you have it all summed up in this superbly colorful dish. If you use fresh pesto, it does take a little time and effort to prepare, but then what else will you have to do but sit back with family and friends and enjoy!

2 packages agar agar
1 x Spicy Tomato Sauce recipe (see page 81)
10 red peppers
20 large spinach leaves, washed and stalks removed
4 large eggplants
4 fennel bulbs
6 large zucchini, cut in quarters lengthways
15 large ripe plum tomatoes, skinned and seeds removed
1 x Pesto recipe (see page 82)

Preheat the oven to 475°F.

Add the agar agar to the warm tomato sauce, following the manufacturer's instructions.

Roast the red peppers for 10 minutes until the skins are blackened. When cool enough to handle, skin, remove seeds, and slice. Reduce the oven temperature to 350°F.

Blanch the spinach for 10 seconds in boiling salted water, refresh in cold water, then dry using a clean dish towel.

Wrap the eggplants in aluminum foil and bake for 30 minutes. Allow to cool, then slice.

Cook the fennel bulbs in boiling salted water for 15 minutes, refresh in cold water, then slice finely.

Pan-fry the zucchini in a little oil or margarine until golden.

Line a 9½ x 4-inch terrine mold or rectangular bread

❋ Chef's Tip

Fresh pesto begins to lose some of its strength after about two hours—for maximum flavor impact, serve about 20 minutes after preparing.

pan with plastic wrap, and then with some of the blanched spinach leaves, overlapping the leaves.

Put a ladle of warm tomato sauce in the bottom of the mold, then a layer of eggplant. Add another ladle of warm tomato sauce, followed by a layer of red pepper.

Continue with a ladle of warm tomato sauce, followed by the zucchini; a ladle of warm tomato sauce then the tomato; and a ladle of warm tomato sauce, followed by fennel, finishing with the spinach.

Cover with plastic wrap, put a weight such as a small chopping board on top of the mold, and refrigerate for at least 24 hours.

To serve, lift the terrine out of the mold using the plastic wrap to help you. Heat the blade of a knife in hot water, cut a slice, and place in the middle of a "pool" of pesto on a large cold plate.

50

Warm Spinach and Mushroom Tartlets with Spicy Tomato Sauce

Serves 4

2–3 bunches fresh spinach, washed and stalks removed
1½ cups mushrooms, washed and sliced
2 tablespoons margarine
½ cup soy milk
3 eggs
1 bunch chives, chopped
salt
1 x Spicy Tomato Sauce recipe (see page 81)

≈

FOR THE PASTRY
2 cups all-purpose flour
1 level teaspoon salt
11½ tablespoons margarine, cut into pieces
1 egg
2 teaspoons water

Make the pastry by putting the flour, margarine, and salt in a food processor, then pulse until it resembles breadcrumbs. Add the egg and water and pulse again until a dough has formed. Wrap in plastic wrap and allow to rest for 2 hours.

Preheat the oven to 425°F.

Roll out the pastry on a lightly-floured surface and use to line four 4-inch tartlet cases. Bake blind for 20 minutes (see page 151). Reduce oven temperature to 375°F.

Blanch the spinach in boiling salted water for 2 minutes, drain, allow to cool, then dry with a cloth. Sauté the mushrooms in the margarine. Leave to cool.

Whisk the milk, eggs and most of the chives together with a large pinch of salt. Divide the spinach and mushroom between the four tartlets and pour over the egg mixture.

Bake until just set—about 10 minutes. Serve on a bed of leaves with the tomato sauce; garnish with chopped chives.

Tartar of Smoked Salmon

Serves 4–6

14 ounces smoked salmon, in a piece
1 cucumber
8 small plum tomatoes, skinned and seeds removed
1 avocado
½ cup mayonnaise (see page 82)
1 bunch dill, finely chopped
1 bunch chives, finely chopped

Cut the smoked salmon into ⅛-inch thick slices and then dice into ⅛-inch cubes. Peel the cucumber, cut in half lengthways, and remove the seeds. Slice one half very thinly. Dice the other half into ⅛-inch cubes. Dice the tomato and avocado in the same way.

Mix together mayonnaise and herbs. Use half of this to bind together the diced ingredients. Divide the mixture into 4–6 pastry cutters.

Spread the remaining mayonnaise with herbs on top of the salmon mixture, and garnish with the sliced cucumber. Chill for 4 hours until set. Place one cutter on each plate, loosen the sides with a knife, and carefully lift off.

Serve with toasted bread.

51

Pasta and Risottos

Opposite: Linguine of Slow Roasted Vegetables

Tagliatelle with Wild Mushrooms and Artichokes

Serves 4

4 tablespoons olive oil
4 tablespoons diced shallot
1 clove garlic, diced
5½ cups wild mushrooms, diced
4 large artichokes, trimmed and outer leaves discarded
1¾ pounds fresh tagliatelle
4 tablespoons chopped chives
pinch of picked thyme
pesto oil and fresh basil to garnish

Heat the olive oil in a pan and fry the shallot, thyme, and garlic until golden. Add the wild mushrooms and continue to fry until these too are golden.

Cook the artichokes in boiling salted water for 10 minutes until tender. Drain, then refresh in iced water. Peel off the leaves, remove the choke and slice. Add to the mushroom mixture.

Cook the tagliatelle according to instructions.

Toss all the ingredients together, then divide between four bowls. Garnish with a drizzle of pesto oil and shredded basil leaves .

Linguine of Slow Roasted Vegetables

Serves 4 – 6

3 small or 2 medium vine tomatoes
12 cloves garlic
¾ cup green beans
4 red peppers
4 yellow peppers
4 baby eggplants
4 baby fennel bulbs
4 small zucchini, cut into julienne strips
½ cup olive oil
3 tablespoons balsamic vinegar
7 ounces fresh linguine

Preheat the oven to 375°F.

Leave the tomatoes whole, including the stalks. Peel the garlic cloves. Cut all the other vegetables to a uniform size so they will cook evenly. Mix well with the oil and vinegar in a roasting pan, and roast for 45 minutes.

Cook the pasta according to instructions, drain well, twist around a fork, and place in the middle of a large warm platter. Spoon the roasted vegetables around the outside and drizzle over the cooking juices.

❉ See picture on page 52

❉ Chef's Tip

To enhance both the flavor and the aesthetics of the linguine, you can drizzle pesto oil and Spicy Tomato Sauce (see page 81) over the pasta.

Opposite: Slow Roasted Vegetables

NEW JEWISH CUISINE

Open Ravioli of Salmon with Chive Velouté

Serves 4

This delicate-tasting dish can be served as either a starter or as the main course. The use of soy milk does not impair the flavor and means it can be served with a meat meal. It's also a useful healthy alternative for anyone opting for a dairy-free diet.

14 ounces salmon, thinly sliced
1 bunch of chives, finely chopped

≈

FOR THE PASTA DOUGH
3½ cups bread flour
5 eggs
1 tablespoon salt
2 tablespoons olive oil

≈

FOR THE VELOUTÉ
3½ tablespoons margarine
⅓ cup plus 1 tablespoon all-purpose flour
2 cups soy milk
salt and pepper to taste

To make the pasta, place all the ingredients for the dough in a food processor and blend until the mixture resembles fine breadcrumbs. Turn out on to a lightly-floured surface and knead until smooth. Wrap in plastic wrap and allow to rest for 2 hours.

Using a pasta machine, roll out the dough until it is paper-thin (or use a rolling pin on a lightly-floured surface). Cut into 20 squares of 2 inches each.

Opposite: Open Ravioli of Salmon with Chive Velouté

To make the velouté, melt the margarine in a pan, then add the flour and stir until thickened. Add the milk, a little at a time, stirring continuously until all the milk has been absorbed and you have a smooth sauce. Continue stirring while simmering for 5 minutes, then strain into a clean pan. Season to taste.

Blanch the pasta squares in boiling salted water for 2 minutes, then drain well.

Preheat the broiler. Arrange the slices of salmon on top of the pasta squares in a warmed large, shallow dish. Flash the salmon and pasta squares under the grill for 1 minute or until the salmon turns opaque.

Bring the sauce back to a boil, add most of the chives, then spoon over the ravioli, and serve with a sprinkling of chopped chives.

✳ Style Tip

Best served in shallow soup plates for eye appeal and easy eating.

57

Pumpkin Risotto

Serves 4

1 tablespoon olive oil
3½ tablespoons margarine
1 clove garlic, finely chopped
2 shallots, diced
2¼ cups pumpkin, skinned, seeds removed, and diced
1½ cups arborio rice
1 cup dry white wine
5¼ cups chicken stock (see page 80)
chives to garnish

Heat the olive oil and margarine in a large pan and sweat the shallots and garlic until soft, then add the pumpkin and cook for 5 minutes or until tender.

Add the rice and the wine to the pumpkin mixture and cook for a further 5 minutes.

Add the chicken stock a ladle at a time, stirring continuously and waiting until all the liquid has been absorbed before adding more. Do this for 15–20 minutes, until the rice is just cooked.

Garnish with chopped chives and serve immediately.

✳ For a fun effect, you can serve this in a hollowed-out baby squash.

Vegetable Risotto

Serves 4

2 tablespoons olive oil
3½ tablespoons margarine
2 shallots, finely diced
2 cloves garlic, chopped
1½ cups arborio rice
1 cup dry white wine
1 red pepper, peeled and diced
1 eggplant, diced
5¼ cups vegetable stock (see page 79)
1 zucchini, chopped
2 plum tomatoes, diced
chives to garnish

Heat the olive oil and margarine in a large pan and sweat the shallots and garlic until soft. Add the rice and the wine and cook for a further 5 minutes.

Add the pepper and eggplant and cook for 5 minutes or until tender.

Add the stock, a ladle at a time, stirring continuously, and waiting until all the liquid is absorbed before adding more. Do this for approximately 10 minutes.

Add the rest of the vegetables and continue to ladle the stock for 5–10 minutes, until the rice is just cooked.

Serve sprinkled with chopped chives.

59

Wild Mushroom Risotto (see recipe page 61)

Wild Mushroom Risotto

Serves 4

Most supermarkets now stock extremely good packages of mixed mushrooms offering an interesting selection of wild varieties that are ideal for this dish. If you choose your own, then make sure you mix for flavor (such as chanterelles), color (try field mushrooms), and shape (for instance trumpet mushrooms). The mushrooms must, of course, be scrupulously clean to ensure that the dish is kosher.

2 shallots, finely chopped
1 clove garlic, finely chopped
¾ cup arborio rice
3½ cups mixed wild mushrooms, wiped clean and sliced
1 cup dry white wine
3 cups vegetable stock (see page 79)
½ cup olive oil
squeeze of lemon juice
chopped chives to garnish

Sweat the shallots, garlic, and rice in 3 tablespoons of the olive oil until transparent, then add half the wild mushrooms.

Add the wine and reduce temperature. Add the vegetable stock to the rice, a ladle at a time, stirring continuously, and waiting until all the liquid has been absorbed before adding more. Do this for at least 20 minutes, or until the rice is just cooked and the liquid is mostly gone.

While the rice is cooking, sauté the remaining mushrooms in 1 tablespoon olive oil.

Mix the sautéed mushrooms into the risotto. Drizzle with the remaining olive oil and a squeeze of lemon juice, garnish with chopped chives, and serve.

Opposite: Wild Mushroom Risotto

Chef's Tip

Be gentle and don't stir the mushrooms too vigorously during cooking to ensure they retain their shape

62

Potato Gnocchi with Sorrel

Serves 4

This dish does take a little effort, but you'll end up with something far superior to the pre-packaged supermarket offerings—and you'll have the satisfaction of serving your guests with the genuine homemade article. One to try and practice, experimenting with shapes and sizes to suit your taste.

FOR THE GNOCCHI

5–6 medium baking potatoes
2 egg yolks
¾ cup all-purpose flour
salt and freshly ground black pepper

≈

4 tablespoons olive oil
2 tablespoons margarine, diced
15 large sorrel leaves, finely sliced

Preheat the oven to 375°F. Bake the potatoes for 1 hour 15 minutes until soft. Take them out of the oven and, when cool enough to handle, scoop out the potato into a bowl. (Keep the skins to use another time: for example, deep-fry and dip in Garlic and Dill Mayonnaise, see page 83.)

Add the egg yolks and flour, and mash until very smooth. Turn out onto a work surface and knead until you have an elastic dough.

Roll out the dough to a thickness of about ¼ inch. Cut out olive-shaped pieces, then roll these with a fork to form gnocchi.

Cook the gnocchi in barely simmering water in small batches for 10 minutes. Drain well.

Toss in a hot frying pan for 2 minutes with the margarine and sorrel. Drizzle with olive oil before serving.

Opposite: Vegetable Lasagne

Vegetable Lasagne

Serves 4 – 5

FOR THE WHITE SAUCE

7 tablespoons margarine
¾ cup all-purpose flour
4¼ cups soy milk
salt, pepper, and 1 teaspoon English mustard to season

≈

4 red peppers
3 zucchini, thinly sliced
2 eggplant, thinly sliced
oil or margarine for frying
1 x Spicy Tomato Sauce recipe (see page 81)
7 ounces lasagne sheets

63

Preheat the oven to 475°F.

To make the white sauce, melt the margarine in a pan over a medium heat, add the flour and stir until thickened. Add the milk, a little at a time, stirring continuously until all the milk has been absorbed and you have a smooth sauce. Add seasonings. Bring to a boil, turn heat down to a simmer for 10 minutes, stir sauce regularly, then strain into a clean pan.

Roast the peppers in a broiler pan for 10 minutes. When cool enough to handle, remove the blackened skins and the seeds, and cut into slices. Reduce oven to 400°F.

Fry the eggplant slices a few at a time in margarine or oil until golden, then drain them on paper towel, and set them aside. Repeat the process with the zucchini slices.

Place a layer of zucchini, eggplant, and red pepper slices on the bottom of an ovenproof dish, cover with a ladle of tomato sauce, then with a sheet of pasta, and then with a layer of white sauce. Repeat these layers until all the ingredients have been used up. Finish by covering the lasagne with white sauce.

Bake for approximately 45 minutes, checking with a skewer to ensure it has cooked thoroughly.

Pesto Tortellini

Serves 4

FOR THE PASTA DOUGH
3½ cups bread flour
5 eggs
1 tablespoon salt
2 tablespoons olive oil
≈
1 x Pesto Sauce recipe (see page 82)
6 cups mixed salad leaves, loosely packed

To make the pasta, place all the ingredients for the dough in a food processor and blend until the mixture resembles fine breadcrumbs. Turn out on to a lightly-floured surface and knead until smooth. Wrap in plastic wrap and allow to rest for 2 hours.

Using a pasta machine, roll out the dough until paper-thin (or use a rolling pin on a lightly-floured surface). Cut out the tortellini shapes using a 2-inch cutter, or cut out circles of that diameter.

Place ½ teaspoon of pesto in the middle of each, reserving some of the sauce for later. Fold the pasta over the pesto and seal with a little water. Then shape the pasta around your forefinger.

Blanch the tortellini in boiling salted water for 2 minutes.

Arrange the salad leaves in the middle of the plate and drizzle the remaining pesto over the leaves and around the edge of the plate.

Place the tortellini around the salad, and serve.

❖ *See picture on page 67*

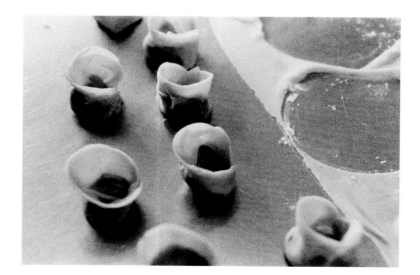

Opposite and above: Making Pesto Tortellini

Mushroom Ravioli with Plum Tomatoes and Truffle Oil

Serves 4

FOR THE PASTA DOUGH

3½ cups bread flour

5 eggs

1 tablespoon salt

2 tablespoons olive oil

≈

FOR THE RAVIOLI FILLING

3½ tablespoons margarine

2 cloves garlic, finely chopped

3½ mixed wild mushrooms, wiped clean and diced

3 tablespoons vegetable stock (see page 79)

≈

8–9 plum tomatoes, skinned, seeds removed, and halved

3 tablespoons olive oil

1 sprig thyme

1 sprig rosemary

1½ tablespoons white truffle oil

fresh basil and cilantro to garnish

To make the pasta, place all the ingredients for the dough in a food processor and blend until the mixture resembles fine breadcrumbs. Turn out on to a lightly-floured surface and knead until smooth. Wrap in plastic wrap and allow to rest for 2 hours.

Preheat the oven to 320°F.

Melt the margarine in a pan and sweat the garlic and mushrooms until soft and well cooked. Moisten with the vegetable stock and cook until thick but not dry.

Place the tomatoes in a baking pan, drizzle over the olive oil and scatter with the thyme and rosemary, then bake for an hour.

Meanwhile, roll out the pasta dough on a pasta roller or a lightly-floured surface until paper-thin, then cut out ten circles per person, using a 3½-inch round cutter.

Put a large teaspoon of the mushroom mixture in the center of one pasta disc, moisten the edges with water, place another pasta disc on top, and then seal by crimping the edges together with your fingers. Repeat until all the pasta and mushroom mixture has been used.

Bring a large pot of salted water to a boil and blanch the ravioli for 4 minutes. Drain carefully and divide between four plates.

Dice the baked plum tomato and sprinkle over the ravioli. Drizzle with the truffle oil and serve immediately.

Garnish with fresh basil and picked cilantro.

Fettuccine with Fresh Pesto and Pine Nuts

Serves 4

1¾ pounds fresh fettuccine

1 x Pesto Sauce recipe (see page 82)

¾ cup toasted pine nuts

1 bunch basil, leaves shredded

Cook the fettuccine according to instructions. Drain and mix with the pesto.

Divide between four bowls, sprinkle with the toasted pine nuts and basil, and serve.

Opposite: Pesto Tortellini

Salads

Opposite: Oriental Smoked Chicken Salad with Sesame and Chili Dressing, and Middle Eastern Tabbouli Salad

Oriental Smoked Chicken Salad with Sesame and Chili Dressing

Serves 4

4 chicken breasts
vegetable oil for frying
2 tablespoons loose tea leaves
2 tablespoons brown sugar
1 teaspoon ground ginger
1 stick lemongrass, chopped
1 bunch cilantro, leaves only
1½–2 cups mixed salad leaves, loosely packed
¾ cup bean sprouts
1 x Sesame and Chili Dressing recipe (see page 84)

Line a wok with a sheet of aluminum foil, then put the tea leaves, sugar, ginger, and lemongrass on top. On top of this, place a wok steamer shelf.

In a separate pan, fry the chicken breasts in a little vegetable oil for 10 minutes until almost cooked, then place them on the steamer tray and cover with the wok lid.

Put the wok on a high heat until it begins to smoke, then turn the heat down very low and continue to cook for a further 10 minutes.

Slice the chicken very thinly.

Mix the cilantro leaves with the bean sprouts and the mixed salad leaves. Dress with some of the Sesame and Chili Dressing, place the chicken on top and then drizzle over the remaining dressing.

❉ Different kinds of tea leaves such as jasmine or lapsang souchong will give their own individual flavors to the smoked chicken.

Middle Eastern Tabbouli Salad

Serves 4

A fusion of colors and flavors make this Middle Eastern salad a classic. Sweet vine plum tomatoes give the best flavor to this dish, which is so versatile I'd be happy to serve it with fish, as a side salad, or to accompany a summer barbecue.

2 red peppers
1 eggplant
1 clove garlic
2 sprigs thyme
1 cup couscous
1 cucumber, peeled, seeds removed, and diced
8 plum tomatoes, skinned, seeds removed, and cut into rounds
1 red onion, finely sliced
1 bunch each of basil and mint, chopped
juice of a lemon
½ cup olive oil
salt and freshly ground black pepper

Preheat the oven to 475°F, then roast the peppers, eggplant, garlic, and thyme for 10 minutes. Allow to cool, then chop finely.

Mix the couscous with 2 cups cold water. Let stand for 15 minutes: the couscous will only absorb as much liquid as it requires.

Mix together the couscous, vegetables, and herbs, add the lemon juice and olive oil, season to taste, and serve.

❉ Chef's Tip

Make an hour before serving to ensure a good blend of flavors. A great chef taught me to make the couscous with cold water to give the salad "bite"—there's no need to cook, it still absorbs the water and doesn't go lumpy.

70

Salad of Broiled Green and White Asparagus with Roasted Red Onions

Serves 4 – 6

A sophisticated salad with the fabulous flavors of sweet red onions, concentrated through roasting and bathed in good-quality balsamic vinegar. Like a fine wine, the best balsamic can be expensive but a good bottle is worth the cost. Something of a modern classic in the kitchen cupboard, it can turn the ordinary into something special.

2 bunches green asparagus (thin or wild)
2 bunches white asparagus (as thin as possible)
12 small red onions
¼ cup brown sugar
½ cup balsamic vinegar
½ cup olive oil
salt

Preheat the oven to 425°F.

Peel the red onions without removing the root, cut in half, and place in a roasting pan. Sprinkle with the brown sugar and drizzle the vinegar over. Roast for 30 minutes.

Blanch the asparagus in simmering water for 2 minutes, then plunge into iced water. When completely cold, drain, then dry thoroughly.

Preheat a griddle pan until very hot. (If you haven't got a griddle pan, you can use a broiler.)

Turn the asparagus in the olive oil, sprinkle with salt, then broil so that it is seared with a criss-cross pattern, taking care not to overcook it.

To serve, place a couple of spoonfuls of roasted red onion on each plate, divide the asparagus between them, then drizzle with the juice from the onions and any remaining oil.

Salade Niçoise

Serves 4

10½ ounces fresh tuna
2 medium new potatoes
1⅓ cups green beans
2 small heads romaine lettuce
4 plum tomatoes, skinned, seeds removed,
    and quartered
4 eggs, boiled and quartered
1¾ ounces anchovy fillets
20 pitted black olives
½ cup olive oil
salt and freshly ground black pepper

Place the tuna under a medium preheated broiler for 5 minutes each side. Allow to cool, then flake.

Boil the potatoes and, when cool enough to handle, cut them into quarters.

Cook the green beans in boiling salted water until tender, then drain thoroughly.

Separate the lettuce leaves, wash them, and dry thoroughly.

Mix together all the ingredients, drizzle over the olive oil, season, and serve.

✻ Set aside some tomatoes and use them to garnish the top of the salad.

71

Smoked Salmon Salad

Serves 4

After more than 20 years in banqueting, I'm still asked for this dish again and again—and why not! Typically Jewish, it is quite simply one of the all-time favorites. There are few more mouth-watering appetizers than choice smoked salmon served with mayonnaise mixed with horseradish to give it a kick.

7 ounces smoked salmon
4–5 small new potatoes
2 tablespoons white horseradish
½ cup mayonnaise (see page 82)
1 bunch chervil
1 bunch dill
4 bunches arugula

Cook the potatoes in their skins then, while still warm, peel, cut into quarters, and mix with 1 tablespoon of the horseradish and half the mayonnaise.

Just before serving, cut the smoked salmon into strips and divide between four plates. Place the arugula leaves on top. Mix the chopped herbs and potatoes with the remaining mayonnaise and horseradish and spoon them around the smoked salmon.

❄ Chef's Tip

Choose only the very best quality smoked salmon, and for a change try serving with slightly warm new potatoes to really bring out the flavor of the fish.

Caesar Salad

Serves 2

1 large head romaine lettuce
4 slices white bread
½ cup olive oil
3 cloves garlic
½ cup mayonnaise (see page 82)
2 ounces anchovy fillets

Separate the lettuce leaves, wash, and dry thoroughly.

Finely dice the garlic. Cut the bread into cubes and fry in the olive oil with the garlic until golden brown. Discard the garlic and drain the croûtons on paper towel.

Mix together the lettuce, mayonnaise, croûtons, and anchovies and serve.

73

Opposite: Smoked Salmon Salad

Roasted Tomato Salad with Herbs

Serves 6

8 medium vine tomatoes
1 sprig thyme
1 sprig rosemary
1 head of garlic, separated into cloves
4 shallots, sliced
1 cup olive oil
1 bunch basil, chopped

Preheat the oven to 475°F.

Wash the tomatoes, then place, together with thyme, rosemary, garlic, and shallots, in a roasting pan. Add the olive oil and mix well, making sure everything is thoroughly coated. Roast for 10 minutes.

Remove from the oven and let cool (if possible leave to marinate overnight). Serve warm, reheating in the oven if necessary, with the basil scattered over the top.

❊ Chef's Tip

Olive oil comes in various strengths and can be diluted with vegetable oils such as corn oil or sunflower oil. Save the best oils for where their flavors will stand out and best complement the food—for example, extra virgin olive oil with this tomato salad.

Artichoke, Avocado, Tomato, and Arugula Salad

Serves 4

1 can sliced artichoke bottoms, drained
2 avocados, skinned, pitted, and diced
8 plum tomatoes, skinned, seeds removed, and diced
8 bunches arugula
3 tablespoons mayonnaise
parsley
chives

Drain the artichokes.

Mix together all the ingredients except the parsley and chives. Serve right away, garnished with picked parsley and coarsely chopped chives.

❊ Chef's Tip

How to skin a tomato: With a small sharp knife, remove the core of the tomato and criss-cross the other end. Plunge the tomato into boiling water for 10 seconds, then plunge it quickly into ice-cold water, and the skin will peel away easily.

Opposite: Roasted Tomato Salad with Herbs

Dips, Sauces, and Dressings

Hummus

Makes 2½ cups

5¾ cups cooked chickpeas
⅞ cup olive oil
½ cup tahini paste
juice of 4 lemons
5 teaspoons ground cumin
8 cloves garlic
salt and freshly ground black pepper

Skin the garlic and pan-fry it in hot oil for a few minutes until browned. Place all the ingredients in a food processor and blend until very smooth.

May be kept in the refrigerator for up to five days.

Salsa

Serves 4 – 6

2 red onions, finely chopped
2 red peppers, finely chopped
2 green chili peppers, finely chopped
1 clove garlic, finely chopped
1 plum tomato, skinned, seeds removed, and finely chopped
3 sprigs cilantro, shredded
1 tablespoon olive oil
juice of 2 limes
1½ teaspoons salt

Mix together all ingredients. Keep in fridge until required.

Guacamole

Serves 4 – 6

2 ripe avocados, skinned, pitted, and finely diced
juice of 1 lime
2 shallots, finely chopped
1 green chili pepper, finely chopped
1 clove garlic, finely chopped
2 plum tomatoes, skinned, seeds removed, and finely chopped
1 tablespoon chopped cilantro
salt and freshly ground black pepper

Bind all the ingredients by mixing them together and season to taste. Eat within a couple of hours, or the avocado will discolor.

Apple and Mustard Chutney

Makes 2½ cups

10 Granny Smith apples
4 tablespoons mustard seeds
1 cup white wine vinegar
1 cup superfine sugar
2 onions, finely chopped
1 tablespoon vegetable oil
zest and juice of 1 lemon
salt and freshly ground black pepper

Sauté the onions in an uncovered frying pan in the oil for a few minutes, stirring constantly. Peel, core, and chop the apples roughly. Place all the ingredients into a large pot with lid and cook gently for 1½ hours until all the excess moisture is reduced. Stir throughout the cooking process.

Add seasoning to taste. Put into sterilized jars and seal. Keep in the refrigerator until needed—up to a month.

Vegetable Stock (Nage)

Makes approx. 2 quarts

½ cup olive oil
2 medium carrots, finely sliced
3 stalks celery, finely sliced
3 small leeks, finely sliced
2 onions, finely sliced
1 fennel bulb, finely sliced
1 head of garlic, separated into cloves
1 bunch dill, roughly chopped
1 bunch parsley, roughly chopped
½ bunch tarragon, roughly chopped
½ cup olive oil
2 bay leaves
20 black peppercorns
3 tablespoons white wine vinegar

In a large pan, gently sweat the vegetables and herbs in the olive oil until tender—about 10 minutes.

Cover with 1 gallon of water, add the bay leaves, peppercorns, and vinegar, bring to a boil and simmer for 5 minutes. Leave to stand overnight.

Strain through a fine sieve and store in the refrigerator for up to four days or in the freezer for up to a month.

Fish Stock

Makes approx. 2 quarts

4½ pounds chopped fish bones (such as sole)
1 carrot, chopped
2–3 stalks celery, chopped
1–2 onions, chopped
2 leeks, sliced
1 head of garlic, separated into cloves
oil or margarine
1¼ cup dry white wine
1 bunch dill, chopped
1 bunch parsley, chopped
1 bay leaf
3 white peppercorns
1 lemon, sliced

Wash the fish bones in cold water, then soak in cold water for 2 hours.

In a large lidded pan, sweat the carrots, celery, onion, leek, and garlic in a little oil or margarine until soft but not colored. Add the white wine and reduce until the liquid is gone, about seven minutes.

Add the fish bones, herbs, peppercorns, and lemon. Cover with cold water and bring to a boil, then simmer for 25 minutes, skimming continuously with a ladle. Strain through a fine sieve.

The fish stock will keep for two days in the refrigerator—or freeze and use within one month.

79

Chicken Stock

Makes approx. 2 quarts

1¼ cups dry white wine
4½ pounds kosher chicken bones, chopped
2 medium carrots, chopped
2 onions, chopped
3 small leeks, sliced
3 stalks celery, chopped
1 head of garlic, separated into cloves
1 bunch parsley, chopped
1 bay leaf
3 white peppercorns

Put the wine in a large pan and cook until it has reduced by three-quarters, so that the alcohol is evaporated.

Add all the other ingredients, cover with cold water, bring to a boil then reduce heat to simmer for 2½ hours, skimming continuously with a ladle.

Strain through a fine sieve.

The stock will keep for two days in the refrigerator, or for a month in the freezer.

✳ For a fuller flavor, you can make a *brown chicken stock* by first browning the bones and vegetables in a very hot oven (475°F) for 30 minutes.

Lamb Stock

Makes approx. 2 quarts

4½ pounds kosher lamb bones
3 small leeks, washed
3 stalks celery, washed
1 onion
2 medium carrots
2 teaspoons tomato paste
1 bay leaf
10 peppercorns
4 sprigs of parsley
2 sprigs of thyme
1 sprig of rosemary

Preheat the oven to 475°F. Roughly chop all the vegetables and place them with the bones in a roasting pan. Put into the oven for 20–30 minutes to brown slightly.

Drain off excess oil.

Place all the ingredients in a large stock pot, cover with cold water, bring to a boil, then simmer covered for 4–6 hours, regularly skimming off any floating residue.

Sieve. Refrigerate and use within 3 days.

Beef Stock

Makes approx. 2 quarts

5 pounds kosher beef marrow bones
2 medium onions, roughly chopped
1½ stalks celery, roughly chopped
1 medium leek, roughly chopped
1 medium carrot, roughly chopped
1 head of garlic, separated into cloves
1 small bunch parsley, roughly chopped
3 bay leaves
20 black peppercorns

Preheat the oven to 400°F, then roast the beef bones for 40 minutes or until dark brown.

Brown the onion, celery, leeks, carrot, and garlic for 10 minutes in a large pan with a little of the fat from the roasted beef bones.

Add the parsley, bay leaves, peppercorns, and beef bones to the browned vegetables. Cover with cold water, bring to a boil and and simmer for 6 hours, topping up with cold water if necessary.

Strain through a fine sieve and store in the refrigerator for up to four days or freeze for up to two months.

❊ Venison or game bones can be used in a similar way.

Spicy Tomato Sauce

Makes approx. 1 quart

4 cloves garlic, finely chopped
4 shallots, finely chopped
3 tablespoons olive oil
16 very ripe plum tomatoes, skinned, seeds removed,
    and cut into quarters
4 mild medium (green) chili peppers, seeds removed, and
    finely chopped
salt and freshly ground black pepper
½ bunch basil, finely chopped
½ bunch cilantro, finely chopped
1 teaspoon cornstarch

In a saucepan, gently cook the garlic and shallots in the olive oil for 5–10 minutes until transparent.

Add the tomatoes and 5 tablespoons of water. Cook gently for 30 minutes on a moderate heat. Then add the chili peppers.

Allow to cool slightly, then purée until smooth.

Add salt and pepper to taste, return to a boil, and adjust consistency by stirring in cornstarch mixed with a little cold water.

Just before serving add the chopped herbs.

81

Pesto

Makes 2 cups

2 large bunches basil
¾ cup pine nuts
2 cloves garlic, chopped
1¼ cups olive oil

Place the basil, pine nuts, and garlic along with all but 1 tablespoon of the olive oil in a food processor and blend until very smooth.

Put into clean airtight jars and pour over the remaining olive oil to prevent air getting to the pesto. Store in the fridge—it will keep for 2–3 weeks.

❋ Cilantro or a mix of herbs of your choice can be used instead of basil.

82

Mayonnaise

Makes 1½ cups

1¼ cups olive oil
2 teaspoons white wine vinegar
2 egg yolks
1 teaspoon Dijon mustard
salt and freshly ground pepper

Whisk the egg yolks, vinegar, and mustard in a stainless steel or glass bowl for a couple of minutes until it emulsifies into a smooth consistency. Slowly add the oil in a continuous stream while continuing to whisk. Once all the oil is used, it should be the correct consistency. If it's too thick, use a little cold water to thin it down. Add seasoning to taste.

Red Wine and Shallot Sauce

Makes 1⅔ cups

15 large shallots, finely chopped
4 cloves garlic, finely chopped
2 bottles full-bodied red wine
1 x brown chicken stock recipe (see page 80)
1 bunch thyme
4 tablespoons ruby port
1 teaspoon cornstarch, if required

Heat the shallots, garlic, and red wine in a large pan and reduce until you have only 1¼ cups of liquid remaining.

Add the brown chicken stock and thyme, and reduce until you have 1⅔ cups of liquid remaining or until syrupy.

Just before serving add the ruby port, but do not boil.

❋ This sauce can accompany all manner of dishes, from roast beef to fish.
❋ Cornstarch can be used to aid thickening—mix it with a little cold water first.

Spicy Peanut Sauce

Makes 3 cups

3½ cups roasted peanuts
⅞ cup margarine
1½ tablespoons soy sauce
3 tablespoons sesame oil
1½ tablespoons mild chili sauce
2 tablespoons honey
1 bunch cilantro, finely chopped

Place the peanuts in a food processor and blend for
5 minutes until you have a very smooth paste.

Add the rest of the ingredients, apart from the cilantro,
and blend again until smooth.

Just before serving, add the cilantro.

Tartar Sauce

Makes 1½ cups

1½ cups mayonnaise (see recipe opposite)
4 teaspoons capers, chopped
¼ cup relish
⅞ cup fresh chopped parsley
salt and white pepper

Make the mayonnaise as opposite. Mix in the other
ingredients. Season to taste.

Garlic and Dill Mayonnaise

Makes 1½ cups

1½ cups mayonnaise (see opposite)
2 cloves garlic, crushed
1 bunch dill, finely chopped
1 dash Tabasco sauce

Make the mayonnaise. Mix in the other ingredients.
Season to taste.

Sweet Chili Dipping Sauce

Serves 6

¾ cup rice vinegar
½ cup superfine sugar
1½-inch piece fresh root ginger
4 bird's-eye chili peppers (small red chili peppers), finely diced
½ medium cucumber, finely diced
½ red pepper, finely diced
1 clove garlic, crushed
1 shallot, finely chopped

In a saucepan, bring to the boil the vinegar, sugar, and
ginger. Reduce by half. (Avoid overcooking as this will
caramelize the sugar.)

Remove from the heat and, while still hot, add the rest
of the ingredients.

Leave to cool so that the flavors infuse before serving.

83

Saffron and Chive Dressing

Makes 2 cups

pinch saffron
½ cup white wine vinegar
salt and freshly ground black pepper
1⅞ cup olive oil
2 bunches chives

Warm the saffron with the vinegar, and a seasoning of salt and pepper, in a pan, but do not allow to boil. Remove from heat and let steep for 10 minutes.

When cool, add the olive oil.

Just before serving, finely chop the chives, add to the dressing, whisk thoroughly, and serve.

Dijon and Balsamic Dressing

Makes 2 cups

4 large shallots, finely chopped
4 tablespoons Dijon mustard
½ cup balsamic vinegar
2 sprigs thyme
¾ cup olive oil
¾ peanut oil

Mix together the shallots, mustard, balsamic vinegar, and thyme leaves and add ½ cup boiling water.

Pour a steady slow stream of the oils into the mustard mixture, whisking continuously, until you have a dressing that resembles runny mayonnaise.

Before serving, whisk once more to emulsify.

84

Sesame and Chili Dressing

Makes 2 cups

⅓ cup white sesame seeds
⅓ cup black sesame seeds
3 green chili peppers, seeds removed and diced
3 red chili peppers, seeds removed and diced
2 cups sesame oil
1 bunch cilantro, chopped

Toast the sesame seeds under a preheated hot broiler until golden.

Mix together the sesame seeds, chili peppers, and sesame oil and leave for two days.

Before using the oil, add the chopped cilantro.

Thyme-flavored Olive Oil

Makes 2 cups

¾ kosher salt
12 cloves garlic
6 small shallots
2 sprigs thyme
2 cups olive oil

Preheat the oven to 300°F.

Sprinkle the salt on a baking sheet then place the garlic and shallots on top with the sprigs of thyme. Bake for 45 minutes until soft to the touch.

While the garlic and shallots are still warm, place the shallots, garlic, and thyme into a jar or bottle and add the olive oil.

Balsamic Vinaigrette Dressing

Makes 2¼ cups

½ cup balsamic vinegar
4 tablespoons whole grain mustard
2 tablespoons dried Herbes de Provence
1¾ peanut oil

Whisk together all the ingredients. Mix well before using.

Lime and Ginger Dressing

Makes 2 cups

zest and juice of 4 limes
1½-inch piece fresh ginger root, grated
1 teaspoon salt
½ cup rice vinegar
¾ cup peanut oil
¾ cup sesame oil

Add the grated ginger, lime zest, lime juice and salt to the rice vinegar.

Whisk the oils into the vinegar.

85

Fish

Opposite: Sea Bass and Salmon en Croûte

Sea Bass and Salmon en Croûte

Serves 4

14-ounce sea bass fillet, thinly sliced
14-ounce salmon fillet, thinly sliced
2¼ pounds puff pastry
4 shallots, finely chopped
2 cloves garlic, finely chopped
1¾ cups mushrooms, finely chopped
½ cup vegetable stock (see page 79)
4 cups fresh spinach, loosely packed
2 eggs

Preheat the oven to 425°F.

Place the shallots, garlic, and mushrooms in a pan with the vegetable stock and cook slowly for 20 minutes until it thickens (this mixture is known as a duxelles).

Blanch the spinach for 1 minute in a pan of boiling salted water, drain, dry with a clean towel, and chop.

Roll out the puff pastry to a thickness of ⅛ inch.

Smooth half the mushroom duxelles over the pastry, to the width of a slice of fish. Cover with a layer of sea bass, then chopped spinach, followed by salmon, and repeat these three layers until all the fish and spinach have been used. Smooth the remaining duxelles of mushroom on top.

Fold the pastry over the filling, seal the edges with a little water, and trim the edges. On a baking sheet, bake in the oven for about 40 minutes until the pastry is golden.

Serve with seasoned vegetables and new potatoes.

❈ *Photograph on page 86*

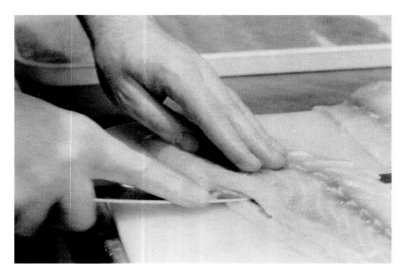

88

89

Sea Bass with Ratatouille and Tapenade Sauce

Serves 4

A contemporary main course you could expect to find on a sophisticated restaurant menu, this dish makes a superb and substantial alternative to a meat main course. The addition of tapenade sauce takes the sea bass to a new taste level.

4 x 5½-ounce sea bass fillets
2 cups spinach (choose thick stocks), loosely packed

≈

FOR THE TAPENADE SAUCE
3½ tablespoons margarine
½ cup pitted black olives
1½ ounces fresh anchovies
2 cloves garlic
1 tablespoon capers
⅓ cup plus 1 tablespoon all-purpose flour
2 cups soy milk

≈

FOR THE RATATOUILLE
3–4 tablespoons olive oil
1 red onion, chopped
2 cloves garlic, chopped
4 red peppers, seeds removed and diced
1 eggplant, diced
8 plum tomatoes, skinned and diced
2 zucchini, diced
salt and freshly ground black pepper
4 tablespoons tomato paste

Make the tapenade sauce by melting the margarine in a pan, add the olives, anchovies, capers, and garlic, and sweat for 5–10 minutes until soft.

Add the flour, and a ladle of cold milk, and mix well. Continue adding the milk, a ladle at a time, stirring constantly, until it has all been absorbed, ensuring that the sauce comes to the boil each time before adding more. Allow to cool slightly, then purée and pass through a sieve. Keep warm.

To make the ratatouille, heat the olive oil in a pan, add the onion and garlic, and sweat until soft. Add the pepper, eggplant, tomato, and zucchini, season with salt and pepper, and cook for about 10 minutes, then add the tomato paste. Continue cooking for a further 5 minutes, taste and adjust the seasoning.

Heat a little oil or margarine in a large pan. Season the sea bass and then fry for 3 minutes on each side.

Place the spinach in boiling salted water for 1 minute. Refresh in cold water. Drain and squeeze out excess liquid. Season with salt and pepper. Mold into cylindrical shapes, one per plate. If desired, reheat in the microwave, covered, for 1 minute.

Place the fish on top of the spinach on the plate with a spoonful of ratatouille beside it.

Reheat the tapenade sauce until boiling, then spoon it around the bass and serve.

Opposite: Sea Bass with Ratatouille and Tapenade Sauce

Halibut with a Potato Crust and Truffled Mashed Potatoes and Spinach

Serves 4

4 x 3½-ounce halibut portions
11–12 new potatoes
4 tablespoons truffle oil
1 truffle, grated
½ cup olive oil
16 cups fresh spinach, loosely packed
salt and freshly ground black pepper
squeeze of lemon

Peel the skins of two of the potatoes and slice thinly. Arrange these slices on top of each halibut portion so they look like fish scales (see tip below).

Peel the remaining potatoes. Cook in boiling salted water until tender, then drain well. Add the truffle oil, 3 tablespoons olive oil, and grated truffle, and mash.

Heat 1 tablespoon olive oil in a large lidded pan. Sauté the spinach leaves over a low heat for 1 minute until wilted, then season with salt and pepper. Keep warm.

Heat the remaining olive oil in a large pan. Season the halibut and fry it, potato side down, over a medium heat for 3 minutes, until golden and crisp, then turn carefully and cook for a further 5 minutes. Add a squeeze of lemon.

Spoon the mashed potato onto warm plates, top it with the spinach, then place the halibut on top, and serve.

✳ Chef's Tip
How to stick the "scales" to the fish:
Dry the flesh of the halibut with paper towel. Brush with egg yolk. Apply the scales. Brush again with egg yolk.
✳ *If you prefer, flavor the mashed potatoes with garlic.*

Baked Sea Bass with Tabbouli Salad

Serves 4

4 x 1 pound 2 ounces sea bass, gutted and cleaned
1 onion, finely sliced
1 fennel, finely sliced
1 lemon, finely sliced
1 bunch thyme, chopped
1 bunch dill, chopped
salt and freshly ground black pepper
½ cup fish stock (see page 79)
1 x Tabbouli Salad recipe (see page 70)

Preheat the oven to 375°F.

If your fishmonger hasn't already done so for you, scale and gut the sea bass, remove the fins, gills, and eyes, then wash well.

Mix together the vegetables and herbs, and place half on a baking sheet.

Slash the flesh of the sea bass with a sharp knife. Fill these "pockets" with some of the remaining herb and vegetable mix, then place the fish on top of the herb and vegetable mix on the baking sheet and put the rest of the herbs and vegetables on top of the fish. Baste with fish stock and season well.

Bake for 30 minutes, checking with a skewer that the middle is hot. If not, return it to the oven for 5-10 minutes.

Serve with the tabbouli.

Opposite: Halibut with a Potato Crust

92

93

Roasted Cod with Baby Vegetables and Pesto Mashed Potatoes

Serves 4

4 x 3½-ounce cod portions
12 small fennel bulbs
12 small carrots
12 small leeks
12 small turnips
2 zucchini, cut into julienne strips
¾ cup fish stock (see page 79)
7 tablespoons margarine
1 teaspoon chopped chervil
salt
1 tablespoon olive oil for frying
≈

FOR THE PESTO MASHED POTATOES
3–4 large baking potatoes
1 x Pesto recipe (see page 82)

Preheat the oven to 425°F.

Blanch the vegetables until tender by placing in a large pot of boiling water for 5-7 minutes.

Peel and dice the potatoes. Simmer in salted water for 10 minutes, then drain, and mash. Add the pesto, mix well, and keep warm.

Season the cod portions. Fry briefly on both sides to seal. Place in preheated oven in suitable pan and roast for 10 minutes.

Bring the fish stock to a boil, then add the blanched vegetables, chervil, margarine, and a pinch of salt. Leave for 30 seconds.

Put some of the mashed potatoes on a plate, place the roasted cod on top, and spoon the vegetables and their cooking juices around it.

Individual Fish Pie

Serves 4

7 ounce cod fillet
7 ounce salmon fillet
3–4 baking potatoes
1 tablespoon chopped chives
1 tablespoon chopped dill
≈

FOR THE WHITE SAUCE
3½ tablespoons margarine
⅓ cup plus 1 tablespoon all-purpose flour
1¾ cups soy milk
salt and pepper

Preheat the oven to 375°F.

Peel and dice the potatoes. Simmer in salted water for 20 minutes, then drain, and mash.

Cook the fish under a preheated medium broiler for 5 minutes on each side.

Melt the margarine in a pan, add the flour, and stir over a low heat for 5 minutes until cooked.

Add the milk, a little at a time, bringing the sauce to the boil each time before adding more. When all the milk has been added, season with salt and pepper, and simmer for 10 minutes, stirring occasionally. Allow to cool.

Cut the fish into chunks and mix it with the white sauce and herbs. Divide between four small ovenproof dishes.

Pipe the mashed potato on top, or smooth over with the back of a fork, then bake for 30 minutes until golden.

Opposite: Roasted Cod with Baby Vegetables and
Pesto Mashed Potatoes

95

Seared Tuna with Arugula and a Lime and Ginger Dressing

Serves 4

A modern-day classic and an appealing alternative to the more traditional choice of salmon, tuna is now seen on every restaurant menu. Meaty enough to tempt even confirmed carnivores, yet with a nice clean taste of the Mediterranean, here it is brought bang up-to-date with the zingy dressing of lime and ginger.

2–3 new potatoes
1 x Lime and Ginger Dressing recipe (see page 85)
4 x 3½-ounce tuna steaks
1 tablespoon oil
4 bunches arugula

Boil the new potatoes in salted water for 20 minutes until cooked but firm, then cut them in half lengthways. Heat the oil in a broiler pan until very hot, then broil the potatoes, searing the cut surfaces with a criss-cross pattern. Place in a bowl and drizzle over a little of the dressing.

Make criss-cross cuts on the tuna steaks and broil quickly on both sides, leaving them pink in the middle.

Mix the arugula with the potatoes and some more of the dressing. Season. Divide between four large plates, place the tuna steaks on top and drizzle over a little more of the dressing.

❈ Chef's Tip

Buy your tuna from a quality fish market, ask for blue fin—a dark purple in color with a strong texture—and cook the same day. Don't be tempted to use frozen, it holds too much water and breaks down in cooking.

Salmon Fish Cakes with Arugula and Pesto

Serves 6

1-pound salmon fillet
1–2 medium potatoes
1 bunch chives, chopped
1 bunch dill, chopped
1 bunch parsley, chopped
≈
4 tablespoons seasoned flour
2 eggs, beaten
2 cups dried breadcrumbs
≈
4 bunches arugula, washed and dried
1 x Pesto recipe (see page 82)

Peel and dice the potatoes. Simmer in salted water for 20 minutes, then drain, and mash.

Cook the salmon under a preheated medium broiler for 5 minutes on each side. Cool and flake.

Mix together the salmon, mashed potato, and herbs, then roll into lime-sized balls, flatten, and chill in the refrigerator for an hour.

When the fish cakes have chilled, roll them in the flour, dip in the beaten egg, and then coat with the breadcrumbs, trying not to alter their shape. Chill for a further 30 minutes, then coat again in breadcrumbs.

Heat a deep fryer to 350°F and fry the fish cakes until golden, about 4–5 minutes.

Serve the fish cakes with the arugula dressed in pesto.

❈ You can chill the fish cakes quickly by putting them in the freezer for 15 minutes, but make sure they don't start to freeze.

96

Assiette of Salmon— Teriyaki, Smoked, & Gravlax —with Oriental Salad

Serves 4

Sounds complicated, but couldn't be simpler. This trio of flavored salmon served with a side salad straight from Asia will keep the traditionalists happy yet still appeal to the more adventurous guest. It is a superb mix of flavors, quickly and easily assembled ready for serving.

3½ ounces smoked salmon,
thinly sliced
3½ ounces gravlax, thinly
sliced (see page 19)
1 bunch arugula
1 bunch cilantro
1 bunch dill
4 heads baby bok choy
1 x Sesame and Chili
Dressing recipe
(see page 84)
≈

FOR THE TERIYAKI SALMON
4 x 2-ounce salmon fillets,
with their skin on
½ cup teriyaki sauce

✳ Chef's Tip

Prepare the teriyaki salmon and gravlax a day before serving so the salmon absorbs the flavor of the marinades.

To make the teriyaki salmon, place the salmon in a bowl with the teriyaki sauce and marinate for 4–6 hours.

Preheat the oven to 400°F and bake the salmon, on a baking sheet, for 20 minutes. Then leave it to cool.

Dress the salad and herbs with some of the Sesame and Chili Dressing, then arrange in the center of four plates. Arrange the slices of smoked salmon, gravlax, and teriyaki salmon around the salad leaves and drizzle with some more of the dressing.

Dressed Salmon with Cucumber

Serves 8–10

1 x 9-pound salmon, gutted and cleaned
1 large cucumber
⅝ cup mayonnaise (see page 82)
≈

FOR THE COURT BOUILLON
1½ tablespoons salt
1 medium carrot
3 bay leaves and 4 parsley stalks
½ cup white vinegar
20 white peppercorns
1 medium onion

Place all the ingredients for the court bouillon in a large pot, add about 1 gallon water, bring to a boil, simmer for 40 minutes, then strain into a clean pan.

If your fishmonger hasn't already done so, scale and remove the fins, eyes, and gills from the salmon. Wash well.

Place salmon in the court bouillon, bring to a boil, and simmer for 15 minutes. Turn off heat and leave the fish to cool in the court bouillon. When cool, lift out the salmon and carefully remove the skin and brown meat under the skin.

Slice the cucumber very thinly. Coat the salmon with a thin layer of mayonnaise and place one on a large salver. Arrange cucumber slices on the fish as if they were scales. Serve with mixed salad leaves, new potatoes, and mayonnaise.

97

Meat and Poultry

Opposite: Roast Rack of Lamb with Pommes Anna

Honey and Mustard Roasted Poussin with Root Vegetables

Serves 4

2 poussins
2 small parsnips
1 rutabaga
1 celeriac
2 large carrots
1 large baking potato
1 large sweet potato
4 tablespoons whole grain mustard
4 tablespoons honey
2 cups brown chicken stock (see page 80)
2 tablespoons vegetable oil
sprig of flat-leaf parsley

Preheat the oven to 425°F.

Pour the stock into the base of the roasting pan. Rub the poussins with the mustard, drizzle over the honey, and roast for 45 minutes.

Peel and chop all the vegetables into ½-inch cubes, discarding the woody core of the parsnips. Blanch the rutabaga, celeriac, carrots, and potato in boiling salted water until tender (about 3–4 minutes), drain, and dry thoroughly. Add the parsnip and sweet potato, then sauté in the vegetable oil for 10 minutes. They are now ready to serve and can be kept in a warm place. Add the parsley, roughly chopped, just before serving.

After the poussins have been roasting for 45 minutes, check that they are cooked by lifting them up with tongs. If the juices don't run clear, return to the oven for another 10 minutes. If the juices run clear, the poussins are cooked, in which case leave them to rest in a warm place wrapped in aluminum foil on a wire rack.

In the roasting pan, skim the fat then reduce the cooking liquid over the heat until you are left with about 1 cup. Sieve and keep warm.

Serve one breast, one leg, and one thigh per person, with the vegetables and some of the sauce.

100

Opposite: Honey and Mustard Roasted Poussin with Root Vegetables

102

Thai Chicken Curry with Basmati Rice

Serves 4

1 x 3½-pound chicken, jointed (8 pieces)
1 tablespoon sesame oil
1 cup basmati rice

≈

FOR THE MARINADE
4 sticks lemongrass, chopped
juice of 4 limes
6 lime leaves
4 cloves garlic, crushed
2 bunches cilantro (roots on)
1 bunch basil
2 green chili peppers
½ cup sesame seed oil
⅞ cup coconut milk
¾ cup chicken stock (see page 80)

Put all the ingredients for the green curry marinade into a food processor and blend for 5 minutes until smooth. Put in a bowl, add the chicken, making sure it is well coated with the marinade, and leave overnight in the refrigerator.

Preheat the oven to 375°F.

Remove the chicken pieces and gently pan-fry in sesame oil in a wok or large frying pan until sealed but not browned. Then put the chicken and the marinade into an ovenproof dish and bake for 2½ hours, turning the chicken in the sauce every 15 minutes.

Just before the chicken is cooked, cook the basmati rice (after having rinsed with water at least two times to remove excess starch) in 6 cups boiling salted water for 12 minutes, drain, and serve with the chicken.

Opposite: Thai Chicken Curry with Basmati Rice

Poached Chicken Supreme with Lemongrass and Sorrel Velouté

Serves 4

4 chicken breasts, with wings attached
4¼ cups chicken stock (see page 80)
4 sticks lemongrass
20 large sorrel leaves
⅔ cup basmati rice
8–9 cups spinach, loosely packed, washed and stalks removed
5½ tablespoons margarine
⅓ cup plus 1 tablespoon all-purpose flour

Rinse rice at least two times in cold water to remove excess starch and prevent it sticking together, then cook in 8 cups salted water for 12 minutes. Drain and cool.

Cook the spinach in boiling salted water for 1 minute, drain, plunge into iced water, and drain again.

Bring the chicken stock to the boil, turn down to simmer, add the lemongrass, half the sorrel leaves, and the chicken, and poach for 15 minutes. The stock should just cover the chicken breast. Remove the chicken, keep warm, and boil the poaching liquid until it is reduced by half.

Melt 3½ tablespoons of margarine in a pan, add the flour, and cook for a minute or so. Gradually add the poaching liquid, stirring continuously, until you have a smooth sauce. Cook for 5 minutes, then strain the velouté through a fine sieve.

Toss the spinach with 2 tablespoons of margarine in a hot wok or frying pan. Drop the rice into boiling water to reheat, then drain.

Divide the spinach and rice evenly between four plates and place the chicken breasts on top of the spinach.

Finely slice the remaining sorrel and add to the velouté. Pour it over the chicken breasts and serve.

103

Confit of Duck with Parsnips and Sweet Potatoes

Serves 4

This robust, rustic-style dish is full of wonderful flavor and should satisfy even the heartiest appetite. It is a classic peasant meal that can be made days in advance, leaving the duck in the fat, and is best enjoyed with granary bread, a rich burgundy, and plenty of time to relax afterward!

4 large duck legs

6 cups duck fat (available from your butcher)

3 medium sweet potatoes, cut into long wedges

2 medium parsnips, cut into long wedges

2 tablespoons honey

4 bunches arugula

1 x Red Wine and Shallot Sauce recipe (see page 82)

≈

SALTING INGREDIENTS

1¾ cups flaked sea salt

4 bay leaves

4 sprigs thyme

4 sprigs rosemary

zest of an orange

12 juniper berries

Mix together the salting ingredients, rub over the duck legs, and leave overnight.

When ready to use the duck legs, wash off all the salt and herbs, and dry thoroughly.

Heat the duck fat in a covered pan, put in the duck legs, and simmer for 2½ hours. Allow to cool in the fat.

Preheat the oven to 475°F.

Take some of the duck fat and simmer the parsnips and sweet potatoes in another covered pan for 8 minutes.

Remove the duck legs from the fat, wipe off any excess fat, put them in a roasting pan, and drizzle with some of the honey. Roast in the oven for 10 minutes until crisp.

In some more of the duck fat, fry the parsnips and sweet potatoes with the remaining honey until caramelized.

Warm the red wine sauce.

Heap a little pile of the root vegetables at one side of the plate, then place some of the arugula at the other. Sit the duck confit on the salad and drizzle with the Red Wine and Shallot Sauce.

✳ Chef's Tip

The "confit" method was devised as a way of preserving meat before the days of refrigeration. Today it is used to intensify the flavors in the dish and is perfect for making several days in advance.

Opposite: Confit of Duck with Parsnips and Sweet Potatoes

104

Noisettes of Lamb with Potato and Parsnip Rosti

Serves 6

1 pound 2 ounces loin of lamb
3–4 new potatoes
1 medium parsnip
5 tablespoons margarine
3 tablespoons olive oil
salt
2 cups lamb stock (see page 80)
10 plum tomatoes, skinned, seeds removed, and diced
5 sprigs thyme
1–2 cloves garlic, crushed

✳ Chef's Tip

How to skin tomatoes:
With a small sharp knife,
remove the core of the tomato
and criss-cross the other end.
Plunge the tomato into
boiling water for 10 seconds,
and then plunge quickly into
ice-cold water and the skin
will peel away easily.

Ask your butcher to cut the lamb into noisettes, removing all the fat and gristle, and then to flatten them a little.

Preheat the oven to 375°F.

Grate the potatoes and parsnip, and mix with a little of the margarine and olive oil and a good pinch of salt. Add crushed garlic. In a large, dry, hot frying pan, fry 4-inch rounds of the potato mixture until golden on both sides. (I use a stainless steel mold to maintain their shape while frying.) Then place on a baking sheet and bake in the oven for 10 minutes. Drain on paper towel to remove any excess oil.

Meanwhile, place the lamb stock, together with the diced tomato and thyme, in a pan and simmer until it reduces down to about 1 cup of liquid. Strain through a fine sieve and keep warm.

Pan-fry the lamb noisettes in a little oil or margarine for a minute on each side so that they remain pink.

Place the rosti on four separate, hot plates. Put the noisettes on top, pour the sauce around the outside, and serve.

Roast Rack of Lamb with a Panache of Vegetables and Potatoes

Serves 6

4 x 3-boned racks of lamb (French trimmed)
12–14 new potatoes, cut into ½-inch cubes
salt and freshly ground black pepper
8 sprigs rosemary
½ cup green beans
¾ cup baby carrots
¼ cup zucchini, cut into julienne strips
1 small turnip
1 small leek
1¼ cups snow peas
1½ cups fresh parsley, chopped
2 cups lamb stock (see page 80)
3½ tablespoons margarine

Preheat the oven to 475°F.

Season the racks of lamb with salt and pepper.

Boil the lamb stock until it has reduced to ½ cup.

Wash the cubed potatoes until the water runs clear. Drain and dry thoroughly.

Preheat a deep-fat fryer to 275°F and fry the potatoes for 8 minutes. Remove the potatoes from the fryer but keep the fryer on low.

Pan-fry the racks of lamb in a little oil or margarine in a very hot pan until golden all over, then put them in a roasting pan and roast for 8 minutes with the rosemary.

Remove from the oven, wrap in aluminum foil, and rest on a cooling rack in a warm place for 10 minutes.

Cook the beans, carrots, zucchini, turnip, and leek in boiling salted water for 5 minutes, then add the snow peas and cook for another 2 minutes. Drain and mix with the margarine and a good pinch of salt.

While the vegetables are cooking, increase the heat in the deep-fat fryer to 350°F. Return the potatoes to the fryer for 4 minutes until crisp and golden. Remove and, while still hot, add the parsley to the potatoes.

Divide the vegetables and potatoes between four large, hot plates, arranging them around the outside. Slice each rack of lamb into three chops and place in the middle of the plate. Drizzle with the warm reduced sauce and serve.

107

❋ Style Tip

Scrape the lamb bones very clean before roasting and cover them with aluminum foil for three-quarters of the roasting time to keep them white and achieve a brilliant final presentation of the dish.

Roast Rack of Lamb with Pommes Anna

Serves 4

When you are out to impress, this stunning dish is hard to beat as it is not only delicious but looks great. The use of fresh garlic, rosemary, and thyme infuses the meal with superb flavors. A dinner-party favorite that never fails to stop the show.

2 racks of lamb, 6 bones on each rack
2 cups lamb stock (see page 80)
2 cups lamb fat
1 sprig thyme
1 sprig rosemary
4 cloves garlic
1 sprig thyme
12–14 new potatoes, peeled and thinly sliced
salt
4 baby fennel bulbs
4 baby carrots
⅔ cup green beans
4 baby turnips
3 bunches fresh spinach

Preheat the oven to 375°F.

Heat the lamb stock in a pan until reduced to a syrup. Keep warm.

In another pan, simmer the lamb fat with the rosemary, garlic, and thyme. Leave to cool for 10 minutes.

✳ Style Tip

Serve on a large plate and rest the lamb bones against the stack of Pommes Anna to give height and eye appeal to the dish.

Line the bottom of an ovenproof dish with parchment paper. Cover with a layer of potato, then spread with some of the lamb fat and a pinch of salt. Place another layer of potato on top and continue thus, ending with a layer of potato, until all the potatoes and lamb fat have been used. Bake in the oven for about an hour until tender. Keep warm.

Increase the oven temperature to 450°F, then roast the lamb for 12 minutes —it should be pink.

Meanwhile, cook the fennel, carrots, green beans, and turnips in boiling salted water for 5 minutes or until tender.

Return the Pommes Anna to the oven for a couple of minutes if needed.

Cook the spinach in a little water for 1 minute until wilted.

Serve the lamb with the potato and vegetables, drizzling the syrupy sauce over the lamb.

109

Opposite: Roast Rack of Lamb with Pommes Anna

Carole Sobell's

Corned Beef Sandwich

Serves 6

*A*traditional and much-loved snack that has stood the test of time to become part of classic Jewish cuisine. Great as a light supper, here it is served in the club sandwich style and served with french fries to give a modern feel to an old favorite. It has long been enjoyed as a "Sunday night special" in my home. So just go for the "wow!" factor and make it large!

7 ounces corned beef, thinly sliced
1 loaf rye bread, sliced
margarine
4 plum tomatoes, sliced
10 cups mixed salad leaves
½ cup Garlic and Dill Mayonnaise (see page 83)
5–6 dill pickles
½ x French Fries recipe (see page 26)

Fill each sandwich with five slices of the beef, some salad leaves, and slices of tomato.

Cut each sandwich diagonally in half, secure with a cocktail stick, and garnish with the mayonnaise, dill pickles, and french fries.

✳ Style Tip

Team the corned beef sandwich with generous bowls of crunchy coleslaw and fresh salad for a great casual supper with friends.

Opposite: Corned Beef Sandwich

Lancashire Hotpot

Serves 6

*O*ne of my all-time favorites and a dish I have served to my family again and again. It's a wonderful winter menu item and I have found it's so tasty, it's a great way of getting children to eat vegetables!

4 large lean lamb cutlets
1 tablespoon oil or margarine
2 sprigs rosemary
1 clove garlic
1 medium leek, chopped and washed carefully
1 medium onion, chopped
1 stalk celery, chopped into ½-inch pieces
1 medium carrot, chopped into ½-inch pieces
5–6 new potatoes, peeled and thinly sliced
1 x Lamb Stock recipe (see page 80)

Preheat the oven to 400°F.

Brown the chops in a little oil or margarine in a hot skillet, then put in a shallow roasting pan with the rosemary. In the same skillet, brown the garlic, leek, onion, celery, and carrot, then sprinkle them over the lamb.

Pan-fry the potatoes until golden, then arrange them over the lamb chops, so that the potatoes are like the crust on a pie. Heat the lamb stock in the same pan and pour it over the hotpot.

Bring the hotpot in the roasting pan to a boil on top of the stove, then cook in the oven for 45 minutes.

Serve the hotpot in bowls with good crusty bread on the side.

111

Tsimmes with Dumplings

Serves 6

This can also serve eight as a side dish, although you can never make enough tsimmes for everyone!

A Rosh Hashanah (New Year) speciality, a tsimmes is a very rich, rustic-style stew, here sweetened with golden syrup. It rightly earns its place in classic Jewish cuisine as a recipe that everyone recalls as something Grandmother used to make. Served with the dumplings, it is a substantial special occasion meal—but note that it will be cooking for six hours!

2 pounds brisket, in a piece
14 medium carrots, peeled and cut into ½ inch pieces
4 heaping tablespoons golden syrup
¼ teaspoon white pepper
2 teaspoons salt
1 tablespoon cornstarch
10–12 new potatoes, peeled and cut into large cubes

≈

FOR THE DUMPLINGS (OPTIONAL)
6 tablespoons margarine
1½ cups self-rising flour or 1½ oz all-purpose flour
    plus 1½ teaspoons baking powder
½ teaspoon salt
3–4 tablespoons water

Trim any excess fat from the meat, leaving a thin edging, then cut it into 1½-inch chunks. Put it in a pot with the carrots, barely cover with hot water, then add half the golden syrup, all the pepper, and ½ teaspoon of salt. Bring to a boil, and simmer gently for 2 hours, either on top of the stove or in an oven preheated to 300°F. Periodically skim off the fat or, if possible, chill overnight, so that it can be removed more easily.

Four hours before you want to serve the tsimmes, make the dumplings by rubbing the margarine into the flour and salt until you have a mixture resembling breadcrumbs. Add the water and mix to a soft dough. Shape into dumplings and put them in the middle of a large oval earthenware, enamel, or enameled cast iron casserole dish. Lift the meat and carrots from their cooking liquid with a slotted spoon and arrange around the dumplings. (If you don't have dumplings, simply put the carrots and meat into the casserole.)

Mix the cornstarch with enough water to make a smooth cream, then stir into the cooking liquid from the carrots and meat. Bring to a boil and pour over the carrots and meat.

Arrange the potatoes on top of the carrots and meat, adding extra boiling water if necessary so that they are just submerged. Sprinkle with the remaining salt and golden syrup. Cover and bring to a boil on top of the stove, then transfer to a 300°F slow oven for 3½ hours.

Uncover and taste, adding a little more syrup if necessary. Return to the oven for another half an hour, then serve. The potatoes and dumplings should be lightly browned and the sauce slightly thickened.

Opposite: Tsimmes with Dumplings

113

Beef Wellington

Serves 4

A great British dinner party dish, the spectacle of carving Beef Wellington at the table has been enjoyed for decades. The use of rib eye as an alternative cut to the original fillet ensures that the dish meets Jewish dietary needs and so earns its place in new Jewish cuisine. Perfect for a candle-lit, special-occasion dinner party.

2 pounds rib-eye beef
3 shallots, finely chopped
1–2 cloves garlic, finely chopped
2½ cups mushrooms, finely chopped
2 tablespoons olive oil
1 pound 11 ounces puff pastry
2 egg yolks, beaten with a little salt
≈

FOR THE PANCAKE BATTER
1 egg
1 egg yolk
3 teaspoons olive oil
1 cup soy milk
½ cup plus 2 teaspoons all-purpose flour
≈
1 x Red Wine and Shallot Sauce recipe (see page 82)

Make the pancake batter by mixing together ingredients, except for the flour, until smooth. Then add the flour, and stir until smooth. Pass the batter through a sieve, and allow to rest in the refrigerator for 20 minutes.

Heat a large non-stick frying pan, add a little oil or margarine, wiping it over the surface of the pan with paper towel, pour on a ladle of batter, tipping the pan so that it is evenly coated, and cook for a minute on both sides. Repeat until all the batter has been used, stacking the cooked pancakes separated by pieces of parchment paper on a plate.

In a separate large pan, brown the beef on all sides in a tablespoon of oil, then rest on a cooling rack. Gently cook the shallots, garlic, and mushrooms in a tablespoon of oil until soft and any moisture has evaporated.

Roll out the puff pastry on a lightly-floured surface until you have a very thin rectangular shape of roughly the same length as the beef. Cover the pastry with the pancakes, then spread these with the mushroom mixture. The pancakes will keep the pastry crisp.

Place the fillet of beef on top, then roll up, making sure that the seam is on the bottom. Trim off any excess pastry and rest in the refrigerator for an hour or overnight.

Preheat the oven to 425°F.

Brush the pastry with the beaten egg yolks, then bake for 45 minutes—the beef will be pink in the middle.

Cut the Beef Wellington into slices, allowing two per person.

Gently heat the red wine sauce and drizzle a little around the beef. Serve on a large serving dish, accompanied by green vegetables.

✳ Chef's Tip

Make sure the mushrooms are well drained and the meat is well sealed before wrapping in pastry. This will help to avoid juices seeping through.

114

Traditional Roast Beef with Yorkshire Pudding and Seasonal Vegetables

Serves 6

4½ pounds rib of beef

⅞ cup vegetable oil

salt and freshly ground black pepper

2⅔ cups beef stock (see page 81)

20–24 new potatoes

⅔ cup baby carrots

¼ zucchini

½ cup green beans

1 baby turnip

1 baby leek

⅞ cup snow peas

3½ tablespoons margarine

2⅔ cups beef stock (see page 81)

≈

FOR THE YORKSHIRE PUDDING

¾ cup plus 1 tablespoon all-purpose flour

2 eggs

1 cup soy milk

Preheat the oven to 475°F.

On the stove, boil the beef stock until it has reduced to a little less than 1 cup.

Make the Yorkshire pudding batter by whisking together the flour and eggs with a pinch of salt, add the milk, then strain through a sieve, and allow to rest.

In a large roasting pan, heat half the vegetable oil, season the beef well, and brown on all sides on the stove.

Peel and cut the potatoes into 1-inch squares, boil rapidly in salted water for 4 minutes, then drain and shake vigorously until the edges start to soften.

Put the potatoes round the beef and roast for 45 minutes. Remove the beef, wrap in aluminum foil and allow to rest for 20 minutes in a warm place. Reduce the oven temperature to 450°F.

If the potatoes are not cooked, return to the oven until they are crisp, then keep them warm.

Heat the Yorkshire pudding pan, then add a little vegetable oil and fill two-thirds full with batter mixture. Bake for 5 minutes, then reduce the oven temperature to 375°F and bake for a further 20 minutes.

Cook the carrots, zucchini, beans, turnip, and leek in boiling salted water for 5 minutes, then add the snow peas and cook for another 2 minutes. Drain, mix with the margarine, and keep warm.

Heat up the reduced beef stock. A little cornstarch dissolved in water can be added to thicken the sauce.

Carve the beef into thin slices and serve with the potatoes, vegetables, Yorkshire pudding, and the reduced beef sauce.

115

Desserts

Opposite: Chocolate Truffle Heart with Summer Berry Fruits and Raspberry Coulis

Chocolate Truffle Heart with Summer Berry Fruits and Raspberry Coulis

Serves 4–6
(depending on size of mold)

This romantic dessert will melt any heart. The chocolate truffle is simply wicked, while the fresh fruit and mint freshen the palate, making it a summer afternoon delight. Note that the hearts should ideally be left in the fridge overnight... if you can keep your hands off them!

1 pound 1 ounce dark baking chocolate (70% cocoa solids)
2 cups non-dairy creamer
4 teaspoons cocoa powder
1⅔ cups fresh strawberries
1 cup raspberries
1¼ cups blueberries
1 cup red currants
1 bunch fresh mint

≈

FOR THE RASPBERRY COULIS
1 cup raspberries
1 tablespoon powdered sugar
squeeze of lemon juice

To make the raspberry coulis, blend all the coulis ingredients in a food processor, then pass through a fine sieve.

To make the chocolate truffle hearts, melt the chocolate in a glass bowl on top of a pan of simmering water, taking care not to let it overheat.

Lightly whisk the creamer, then fold in the chocolate, and spoon into heart-shaped molds. Place in the refrigerator to set for at least four hours—and preferably overnight.

Using a warm knife, loosen the chocolate hearts. Dust liberally with cocoa powder and then place each in the center of a white plate.

Garnish with strawberries cut in quarters, raspberries, blueberries, red currants, and sprigs of fresh mint.

Drizzle raspberry coulis over the fruits.

❋ *See picture on page 116*

118

Crêpe Suzette with Oranges and Caramel

Serves 4

I am always asked to include this classic on dessert buffets at banquets—and it's still as delicious as it always has been. The great thrill is to see the chef flambé the crêpes at the table—which is said to be the way it was originally served at the Café de Paris in France—but they are just as good made in advance and brought back to heat with the warmed sauce.

FOR THE CRÊPE BATTER
½ cup plus 2 teaspoons all-purpose flour
1 egg
1 egg yolk
4 teaspoons sugar
zest and juice of 2 tangerines
1 cup soy milk
≈
6 oranges, segmented
juice of 6 oranges (and the zest of one)
3 tablespoons brandy
1 teaspoon sugar
⅝ cup powdered sugar

Whisk together the flour, egg, egg yolk, sugar, and tangerine zest and juice, then gradually add the milk, whisking continuously. Leave to rest for 2 hours.

Heat a nonstick frying pan, wipe it with a little oil or margarine using paper towel, then ladle on a spoonful of batter, tipping the pan to ensure it is evenly coated, and cook the crêpe a minute or so on each side. When done, stack the crêpes, with a piece of parchment paper between each crêpe. Keep warm. This amount of batter should make 8–10 crêpes.

Put the brandy in a pan. Light it, using a blowtorch or a match. (It will go out when the alcohol has been burned away, leaving the brandy flavor.) Add the juice of six oranges, the zest of one, and one teaspoon of sugar, and boil until reduced by half to make the caramel sauce.

Dust the orange segments with powdered sugar, then caramelize using a blowtorch or under a preheated hot broiler. Save resulting juices.

To serve, place a crêpe plus some of the orange segments on a plate and then drizzle the juices and the caramel sauce over, then serve.

✳ Chef's Tip
If you want to flambé the crêpes, a safer alternative at home is to take a dish of hot brandy to the table and light at arm's length with a safety match—and don't forget to turn down the lights first!

119

Lockshen Kugel

Serves 6

This traditional pudding, originally made on Fridays and cooked overnight so that it could be served hot on the Sabbath, is quite heavy. To give it a lighter touch and a more modern presentation, I like to cut the long loaf into squares, drizzle with sauce, and garnish with berry fruits. It can be served cold, but is much nicer hot.

The crusty lining, which is the best part of a kugel, comes from heating the margarine in the baking dish and then using it to coat the sides.

4 tablespoons margarine
8 ounces egg noodles, broad or narrow as preferred,
    but no broader than ¼ inch
2 eggs
⅔ cup sugar
pinch of cinnamon
pinch of salt
1 Granny Smith apple, grated
grated zest of ½ lemon
⅓ cup raisins
⅓ cup chopped candied or dried fruit (optional)

Preheat the oven to the preferred temperature (see below). Put the margarine in either a 2-inch deep oven-to-table casserole dish measuring about 8 x 10 inches or a round 7–8 inch soufflé dish, with a liquid capacity of about 1½–2 quarts.

Put this into the oven. Meanwhile, boil the noodles

✱ Style Tip

Serve in the center of a big plate and dust the edges with cocoa powder if using a light-colored plate, or powdered sugar on dark—something of a Sobell signature!

according to instructions, then drain well.

Whisk the eggs and the sugar to blend, then stir in the cinnamon, salt, zest, raisins, apple, and candied or dried fruit, if using. Stir in the noodles. Swirl the melted margarine around the baking dish to coat the sides, then stir it into the mixture.

Pour into the baking dish. Bake either at 375°F for 45 minutes or at 300°F for 1½ hours. In either case it should be set inside and crisp and brown on top.

✱ The kugel can be kept for three days in the refrigerator and for up to three months in the freezer.

Opposite: Lockshen Kugel

Carole Sobell's

Sticky Toffee Pudding with Caramel Sauce and Crème Anglaise

Serves 6 – 8

¼ cup dates, pitted and chopped

16 tablespoons margarine

¾ cup brown sugar

4 eggs, lightly beaten

1 cup all-purpose flour

1 teaspoon baking powder

1 x Crème Anglaise recipe (see page 136)

≈

FOR THE CARAMEL SAUCE

½ cup brown sugar

7 tablespoons margarine

½ cup non-dairy whipped topping

⅓ cup golden syrup

Preheat the oven to 350°F.

Butter and flour four 2-inch ramekins, or individual square baking pans.

Place the dates in a pan with ⅔ cup water, bring to a boil, and simmer for 2 minutes.

Cream the margarine and brown sugar by beating together until light and fluffy.

Gradually add the dates and the eggs to the creamed mixture, then fold in the flour and baking powder.

Spoon into the greased ramekins and bake for 45 minutes or until firm to the touch.

Place all the caramel sauce ingredients in a saucepan, bring to a boil, and simmer for 5 minutes, whisking occasionally.

Serve warm with both the caramel sauce and some crème anglaise.

Individual Chocolate Puddings

Serves 4 – 6

7 tablespoons margarine

¾ cup superfine sugar

3 eggs

1 cup self-rising flour

¼ cup cocoa powder

3½ ounces baking chocolate (70% cocoa solids), grated

Lightly grease four 1-cup ramekins with a little margarine.

Cream the margarine and sugar by beating together until light and fluffy.

Lightly beat the eggs. Gradually add the eggs to the creamed mixture, beating continuously as you do so.

Fold in the flour, cocoa, and grated chocolate.

Spoon into the four greased ramekins, cover with aluminum foil, and secure with string.

Place in a steamer, or in a lidded saucepan filled with water to halfway up the bowls. Bring the water to a boil, then turn down to a simmer. Steam for 60 minutes, making sure it doesn't boil dry.

Turn out and serve with crème anglaise (see page 136) or vanilla ice cream (see page 140).

Opposite: Sticky Toffee Pudding with Caramel Sauce and Crème Anglaise

122

Crème Brûlée

Serves 6

2⅔ cups non-dairy creamer
5 large eggs
½ teaspoon vanilla extract
⅓ cup superfine sugar

Preheat the oven to 250°F.

Mix the creamer, eggs, vanilla, and half the sugar in a large bowl, then pour into a baking dish, or individual ovenproof bowls. Place the dish or bowls in a roasting pan with hot water at a depth of 1 inch, then bake in the oven for about an hour or until just firm.

Leave to cool, then refrigerate for at least 4 hours, or overnight. About ten minutes before serving, preheat a hot broiler (unless you plan to use a blowtorch).

Cover the chilled creamer mixture with the remaining sugar, working it through a sieve.

Brown under the broiler for 3 or 4 minutes, or heat with a blowtorch for a minute, until the sugar has melted and formed a golden crust over the custard. Don't do this too early, as the sugar will become soft and lose its crispness.

Leave to cool.

❋ Chef's Tip

A small hand-held blowtorch can be bought at hardware or specialty kitchen stores. It is easy and safe to use, and runs on a small refillable gas bottle.

Opposite: Crème Brûlée

Roasted Pineapple with Vanilla Ice Cream and Chili

Serves 4

For the "wow!" factor, this most modern of desserts has the lot. It blends sweet and succulent pineapple with a surprising tang of chili complemented by the velvety vanilla ice cream. A real treat to take the taste buds from hot and spicy to cool and smooth, it's a guaranteed talking point to complete any dinner party. Presentation can be half the fun of cooking, and this recipe will help you to do it in style.

4 small pineapples, skinned and cored
2 vanilla beans
1 large mild red chili pepper
½ cup sugar
3 tablespoons rum
1 x Vanilla Ice Cream recipe (see page 140)

✳ Chef's Tip

When handling chili peppers, either wear gloves or wash your hands immediately afterward, as they can cause burns and severe irritation if they come into contact with your skin. And don't rub your eyes!

Preheat the oven to 375°F.

To present the pineapple as in the photograph, hold the leaves firmly and twist. This will separate the leaves from the pineapple. Don't throw the leaves away! Remove the lower leaves and with a sharp knife square off the base of the bunch. Retain these for the final presentation. With a sharp knife, remove the top and bottom of the pineapple. Stand the pineapple upright on a chopping board. Shave off the peel. Score the pineapple in a spiral fashion.

Retain all the juice from the peelings to be used in the cooking process.

Cut the vanilla beans and chili peppers into very thin strips, discarding the chili seeds unless you prefer a spicier dish. Stud the pineapples with the vanilla and chili.

In a small ovenproof dish, lightly caramelize the sugar under a broiler or using a blowtorch, then, in order to keep it from overcooking, pour in the rum.

Put the pineapples in the dish, pouring in any juice leftover from the peelings, and roast for 45 minutes, basting five or six times.

Serve with some of the cooking juice and a scoop of vanilla ice cream.

127

Opposite: Roasted Pineapple with Vanilla Ice Cream and Chili

Chocolate Tower with Caramelized Walnut and Honey Delight

Serves 6

FOR THE WALNUT PRALINE
1 cup superfine sugar
2 cups roasted walnuts, halved

To make the walnut praline, place the sugar in a saucepan and heat gently until totally melted and golden brown. Stir in the walnut halves, then spread out on an oiled baking sheet to cool. When cold, blend in a food processor.

≈

FOR THE HONEY DELIGHT
¼ cup superfine sugar
5 egg yolks
2 tablespoons honey
1 cup non-dairy whipped topping
3½ ounces baking chocolate (70% cocoa solids), grated

To make the honey delight, place the sugar in a saucepan with ½ cup of water, bring to a boil, then simmer for 3 minutes. In a mixing bowl, pour this slowly into the egg yolks, whisking continuously until stiff—about 10 minutes. Whisk the whipped topping until it forms soft peaks. Fold in the eggs, chocolate, honey, and walnut praline. Line a bread loaf pan with plastic wrap. Pour in the mixture and freeze for a minimum of 8 hours.

FOR THE CARAMEL SPIRALS
1 cup superfine sugar
1 teaspoon light corn syrup
4 teaspoons water

To make the caramel spirals, mix the sugar and corn syrup in the water and bring to a boil until golden brown. Remove from heat. Allow to cool for 10 minutes. Place spoon in caramel. Lift out, and the sugar will form a thread. Twist the thread of sugar around the handle of a wooden spatula. When this sets, slip off to form sugar spirals. ❋ Take care not to splash your skin; the caramel will burn.

≈

FOR THE CHOCOLATE TOWER
6 ounces baking chocolate (70% cocoa solids)
parchment paper

To make the chocolate tower, melt the chocolate in a glass bowl in the microwave or over hot water. Spread the melted chocolate onto the center of a sheet of parchment paper. Roll the paper into a cylinder, allowing the chocolate to overlap by a about half an inch. Place in the refrigerator for 10–15 minutes. Carefully peel the parchment paper off the chocolate. Using a hot, dry sharp knife, trim the cylinder into six segments, each about 3 inches in length.

≈

To assemble, place the chocolate cylinder in the center of the plate. Fill to three-quarters with scoops of honey delight. Arrange sugar spirals on top. Decorate the plate with melted chocolate and crème anglaise sauce (see page 136).

Opposite: Chocolate Tower with Caramelized Walnut and Honey Delight

Carole Sobell's

NEW JEWISH CUISINE

Assiette of Poached Fruits with Mango and Raspberry Sorbets

Serves 4

2½ cups sugar

4 vanilla beans

4 passion fruit

2 Granny Smith apples, peeled and cored

2 firm William pears, peeled and cored

1 large mango, peeled and stoned

12 large strawberries, hulled

30–35 raspberries

2 kiwi fruit, peeled and sliced

2 peaches, peeled and halved

1 x Mango Sorbet recipe (see page 142)

1 x Raspberry Sorbet recipe (see page 142)

Place the sugar, vanilla beans, and passion-fruit pulp in a large pan with 2 cups water and bring to a simmer. Add the apple and pears and simmer for 3 minutes or until tender. Add the rest of the fruit and simmer for another minute, then cool on a plastic tray, saving the liquid.

In a stem serving glass, serve the poached fruit drizzled with some of the liquid, with the mango and raspberry sorbets.

Tarte au Citron with Seasonal Berries and Raspberry Coulis

Serves 6

8½-inch pastry case baked blind (see page 151)

3¾ cups non-dairy creamer

½ cup sugar

8 large eggs

zest and juice of 6 lemons

2 cups raspberries

1 tablespoon powdered sugar

1⅔ cups strawberries

1 cup red currants

Mix ⅜ cup of the sugar with the eggs and lemon zest and juice for 2 minutes. Add the creamer. Leave to stand for 4–6 hours to intensify the flavor.

Preheat the oven to 250°F.

Sieve the mixture. Pour it into the pastry case and bake for approximately 1 hour until *just* set.

Allow to cool. Do not refrigerate.

To make the coulis, purée one cup of raspberries with the powdered sugar, then pass through a fine sieve.

When the tart is cool, sprinkle with the remaining sugar, and caramelize using a blowtorch or hot broiler, until the sugar bubbles and goes brown. (Do not overcook or you may curdle the tart, and don't touch the caramel as it will be very hot!)

Serve the tart in slices, with some of the berries and a drizzle of the coulis.

130

Assiette Gourmande: Raspberry Sorbet, Passion Fruit Mousse, Chocolate Mousse, and Lemon Tarte with Raspberry Coulis

Serves 4

A firm favorite at banquets, this delightful combination dessert isn't as complicated as it sounds. It is a little time-consuming to prepare but can be made well in advance and assembled on the day. Your efforts will be repaid in the reception it receives, as it looks great and offers something for everyone.

4 slices Tarte au Citron (see opposite)
12 tuile baskets (see Plain Tuiles recipe, page 146)
seasonal berries to garnish
1 bunch mint to garnish

≈

FOR THE RASPBERRY SORBET
5 cups raspberries
⅝ cup powdered sugar
juice of a lemon

≈

FOR THE CHOCOLATE MOUSSE
4 ounces baking chocolate (70% cocoa solids)
⅜ cup non-dairy whipped topping

≈

FOR THE PASSION FRUIT MOUSSE
½ Pastry Cream recipe (see below)
pulp of 4 passion fruit
¼ cup non-dairy whipped topping

≈

FOR THE PASTRY CREAM (MAKES 1¼ CUPS)
½ split vanilla bean
3 egg yolks
¼ cup superfine sugar
3 tablespoons all-purpose flour
1 cup soy milk
pulp of 4 passion fruit
4 tuile baskets (see Plain Tuiles recipe, page 146)

To make the pastry cream, heat the milk with the vanilla bean. Do not boil. In a mixing bowl, stir the eggs with the sugar for 5 minutes. Add the flour and mix again. Pour hot milk into the egg mixture in a steady stream, stirring continuously. Pour the mixture into a clean pan, return to the stove, and stir for 1 minute. Do not boil. Remove and cover with plastic wrap to prevent a skin forming. Pastry cream can be used as a base for fruit tartlets or to fill profiteroles.

To make the raspberry sorbet, purée the raspberries with the powdered sugar and lemon juice, pass through a fine sieve, and churn all but ⅛ cup in an ice cream machine for 15 minutes until firm, then freeze. Chill the reserved coulis.

To make the chocolate mousse, melt the chocolate in a glass bowl, either in the microwave or over hot water. Add in half the whipped topping. Whisk remaining whipped topping to stiff peaks. Fold together. Refrigerate for at least 2 hours.

To make the passion fruit mousse, fold the whipped topping together with the pastry cream and passion fruit pulp to form a light mousse.

On a large white plate, put a small slice of tarte au citron. Place three tuile baskets around the edge of the plate.

Fill one tuile with piped chocolate mousse, another with piped passion fruit mousse, and fill the remaining tuile with sorbet.

Dust with powdered sugar, drizzle with raspberry coulis, and garnish with fresh seasonal berries and mint.

131

Summer Pudding with an Apple Sorbet and Raspberry Coulis

Serves 4

3 cups raspberries
¼ cup superfine sugar
½ loaf white bread, thinly sliced
1⅔ cups strawberries
1 cup blackberries
1 cup red currants
1¼ cups blueberries
1 cup black currants
1 teaspoon of lemon juice

≈

FOR THE APPLE SORBET
8 Granny Smith apples, peeled and cored
⅞ cup powdered sugar
juice of a lemon

To make the apple sorbet, place the apples in a blender with the powdered sugar, lemon juice, and ½ cup of water. Blend, then pass through a fine sieve. Churn in an ice cream machine for 15 minutes until firm, then freeze.

Purée two cups of raspberries with the superfine sugar, then pass through a sieve to make the coulis.

Line four 1-cup ramekins with plastic wrap. Dip the bread in the coulis and use to line the molds, reserving four slices for topping.

Wash and trim the remaining fruit, then mix with the 1 teaspoon of lemon juice and all but 6 tablespoons of the raspberry coulis.

Press the fruit into the lined dishes, top with one more piece of dipped bread, then press between two weighted plastic trays overnight.

Serve the puddings with the apple sorbet and the remaining coulis.

Individual Chocolate Soufflés

Serves 4

4 tablespoons superfine sugar, plus extra for dusting
2 tablespoons all-purpose flour
2 tablespoons Dutch cocoa powder, plus extra for dusting
1 tablespoon cold margarine
½ cup soy milk
2 ounces unsweetened chocolate, finely chopped
1 large egg yolk
2 large egg whites

Grease 4 shallow ramekin dishes (or any small ovenproof porcelain dish with straight sides) and dust them with sugar, shaking out the excess.

In a bowl, blend together half the sugar, the flour, the cocoa powder, and the margarine until the mixture resembles breadcrumbs.

In a saucepan, bring the milk to a boil, then whisk in the sugar and cocoa mixture, together with the chocolate, and cook over a moderate heat, whisking continuously, for 1 minute or until the mixture has thickened. Allow to cool.

Preheat the oven to 400°F.

In a bowl, lightly beat the egg yolk, then beat in the chocolate mixture.

In a separate bowl, beat the egg whites until they hold soft peaks, then add the remaining sugar, a little at a time, continuing to beat the meringue until it holds stiff peaks. Fold a quarter of the meringue into the chocolate pastry cream to lighten it, then gently but thoroughly fold in the remaining meringue.

Divide the mixture between the prepared ramekins and bake for 12–15 minutes.

Dust with cocoa powder and serve immediately.

Opposite: Individual Chocolate Soufflé

132

NEW JEWISH CUISINE

Poached Red and White Pears with Vanilla and Cinnamon

Serves 4

8 very small pears
1 bottle red wine
5 cups superfine sugar
4 star anise
2 vanilla beans, split
4 sticks cinnamon
juice of 2 lemons
⅞ cup crème anglaise (see page 136)
½ teaspoon ground cinnamon

Pour the wine into a large pan, add two cinnamon sticks, one vanilla bean, two star anise, and half the sugar, bring to a boil and simmer for 5 minutes.

In a separate large pan, put 2 cups water and the remaining sugar, cinnamon sticks, vanilla beans, and star anise, plus all the lemon juice. Bring to a boil and simmer for 5 minutes.

Peel and core the pears—keep them whole and retain the stalks. Put four in each pan and simmer until just soft, about 10 minutes. Allow to cool. (The pears may be stored in the cooking liquid in the refrigerator for several days.)

Mix half the crème anglaise with the ground cinnamon.

Cut the white pears in half and make each half into a fan: place flat side down on a chopping board, and cut lengthwise into 15–20 fine slices without severing at the thin end, then press down and the pear will fan out.

Place the red pears upright on large white plates, with the white pears fanned on either the side.

Drizzle over the two crème anglaise sauces and serve.

✽ Garnish with a dusting of powdered sugar, mint sprigs, and red currants.

Pear Tarte Tatin with Vanilla Ice Cream

Serves 4

4 pears
8½ ounces puff pastry
¾ cup superfine sugar
2 tablespoons water
2 vanilla beans, split
1 x Vanilla Ice Cream recipe (see page 140)

Preheat the oven to 350°F. Thinly roll out the pastry on a lightly-floured surface. Cut four 4-inch circles.

Boil the sugar and water together for a few minutes until golden brown. Remove this caramel mixture from the heat and leave to cool for 5 minutes.

Place the sliced vanilla beans in four 4-inch tartlet pans. Pour the caramel on top. Peel and core the pears, and slice them in half. Fan each half into very fine slices. Place the curved side in the caramel. Cover with the puff pastry disc. Bake for 30 minutes, until crisp and golden.

To serve, turn the tarte tatin onto a plate so that the pastry is underneath. Serve warm or cold with ice cream.

✽ Chef's Tip

For a dessert treat, try this Banana Tarte Tatin. Follow the recipe for Pear Tarte Tatin, but use six firm bananas instead of the pears. Slice the bananas fairly thin. Chocolate Ice Cream (see page 140) makes a great accompaniment—the sweetness of the bananas is beautifully offset by the chocolate!

Opposite: Pear Tarte Tatin with Vanilla Ice Cream

Apple and Blackberry Crumble with Raspberry Coulis and Crème Anglaise and Vanilla Ice Cream in a Tuile Basket

Serves 4

A classic turned into a stunningly presented dessert and here adapted for the Jewish table by the use of a non-dairy ice cream so that it can be eaten as part of a meat meal. The combination of colors and textures come together beautifully and are a feast for the eyes.

FOR THE CRÈME ANGLAISE
1¾ cup soy milk
⅜ cup superfine sugar
1 vanilla bean
8 egg yolks
⅞ cup non-dairy creamer

To make the crème anglaise, simmer the soy milk with half the sugar and the vanilla bean. Whisk together the egg yolks, creamer, and the remaining sugar until pale and fluffy. Pour the simmering soy milk (with vanilla bean removed) into the yolk mixture, whisking continuously, then put back on the heat and cook gently, making sure it doesn't boil, until the custard coats the back of a spoon. Strain through a fine sieve and allow to cool.

≈

FOR THE RASPBERRY COULIS
1 cup raspberries
¼ cup powdered sugar

To make the coulis, purée the raspberries with the powdered sugar, then pass through a fine sieve.

4 Granny Smith apples, peeled and diced
1 cup sugar
1 cup blackberries
¾ cup plus 1 tablespoon all-purpose flour
4 tablespoons margarine

≈

1 x Vanilla Ice Cream recipe (see page 140)
4 tuile baskets (see Plain Tuiles recipe, page 146)

Preheat the oven to 325°F.

Put the apple into a pan with ½ cup of the sugar and a little of the margarine, and cook gently until soft. Drain and mix in the blackberries.

Put the flour, along with 3½ tablespoons of margarine and ½ cup of sugar in a food processor and pulse until the mixture resembles breadcrumbs.

Place four 4-inch metal cutters on a baking sheet. Fill them with the warm apple and blackberry mixture, top with crumble, then bake in the oven for 20 minutes until the top is golden.

Put on plates, carefully remove the cutters, drizzle over the raspberry coulis and crème anglaise, and serve with a scoop of ice cream in each tuile basket on the side.

Warm Glazed Plum Tart with Vanilla Ice Cream

Serves 6

14 ounces puff pastry
6 plums
¼ cup plus 1½ teaspoons sugar
1 x Vanilla Ice Cream recipe (see page 140)

≈

FOR THE CRÈME PATISSERIE
2 cups soy milk
⅔ cup superfine sugar
1 vanilla bean, split and scraped out
⅝ cup all-purpose flour
7 egg yolks

To make the crème patisserie, whisk the egg yolks with ⅔ cup sugar, add the flour, and whisk to a pale, thick consistency. Scrape the vanilla bean insides into the milk, then add whole bean. Bring the milk to a boil, then add to the egg yolks and flour mixture, and whisk until blended. Return to the saucepan and set on a low heat. Whisk continually until you have a thick custard. Pour into a tray or bowl and cover with plastic wrap to stop a skin forming. Let it cool down and take out the vanilla bean.

Preheat the oven to 400°F.

Roll out the puff pastry thinly on a lightly-floured surface and use it to line an 8½-inch flan pan. Allow to rest for 20 minutes, then bake blind for 20 minutes (see page 151). Increase the oven temperature to 475°F.

Cut plums in half, pit them, sprinkle with the remaining sugar. Place in a pan and cook for 5 minutes over a moderate heat to draw out some moisture, then drain well.

Spread a ½-inch deep layer of crème patisserie over the bottom of the flan pan. Arrange the plums on top, then bake for 25 minutes. Serve with vanilla ice cream.

Bread and Butter Pudding with Honey Ice Cream

Serves 4

1 medium loaf challah (sliced 2 inches thick, crust on)
6 tablespoons margarine, melted
1 cup non-dairy whipped topping
⅞ cup soy milk
6 eggs
1 cup superfine sugar
1 vanilla bean, split
pinch of salt
1½ tablespoons golden raisins
⅓ cup apricot glaze (melted apricot jam)
powdered sugar for dusting

≈

FOR THE HONEY ICE CREAM
1 x Vanilla Ice Cream recipe (see page 140)
with 2–3 tablespoons of honey churned through the mixture while making the ice cream
1 tuile basket per serving (see page 146)

Mix milk, whipped topping, eggs, sugar, salt, and split vanilla bean. Let stand for 1 hour, then sieve. Grease an earthenware dish with margarine. Brush challah slices with melted margarine, then place in the dish in layers with slices slightly overlapping, sprinkling golden raisins between each layer.

Add the custard mixture on top, making sure the bread absorbs the mixture. Place dish in a large roasting pan half-filled with hot water. Cook for 45 minutes at 325°F. Remove from oven. Brush a thin coating of warmed apricot glaze over the top of the pudding.

To serve, place a ball of ice cream in a tuile basket on a large plate. Cut a 3-inch square of pudding and place in the center of the plate. Dust with powdered sugar. Serve with raspberry coulis and crème anglaise (opposite).

137

Carole Sobell's

Ice Cream and Sorbets

Opposite, from left: Strawberry Ice Cream, Chocolate Ice Cream, Mango Sorbet, Pistachio Ice Cream, and Champagne Sorbet

Vanilla Ice Cream

Serves 6

2 cups soy milk
½ cup superfine sugar
2 vanilla beans, split in half lengthways
6 egg yolks
⅝ cup non-dairy creamer

Heat the milk, half the sugar, and the vanilla beans in a pan and simmer for 2 minutes. Discard the vanilla.

Meanwhile, whisk together the yolks and remaining sugar until pale.

Pour the milk into the egg mixture, whisking continuously. Return to the heat and cook gently, stirring continuously, until it thickens slightly. Cool in a bowl of iced water.

When cold, stir in the cream and churn in an ice cream machine for 15 minutes until firm, then freeze.

❋ You can use the vanilla beans several times. Simply rinse them, wrap them in plastic wrap and keep them in the refrigerator.

Chocolate Ice Cream

Serves 6

2 cups soy milk
½ cup superfine sugar
2 vanilla beans, split in half lengthways
6 egg yolks
⅝ cup non-dairy creamer
3½ ounces dark chocolate (70% cocoa solids), grated

Heat the milk, half the sugar, and the vanilla beans in a pan and simmer for 2 minutes. Discard the vanilla.

Melt the chocolate in a glass bowl set over a pan of simmering water. (Alternatively, melt it in a Pyrex bowl in the microwave, heating it for 10 seconds at a time, stirring and repeating.)

Meanwhile, whisk together the yolks and remaining sugar until pale. Pour the milk onto the egg mixture, whisking continuously, until it thickens slightly.

Add the melted chocolate to this crème anglaise.

Cool in a bowl of iced water. When cold, stir in the cream and churn in an ice cream machine for 15 minutes until firm, then freeze.

140

Chocolate Chip Ice Cream

Serves 6

1 x Vanilla Ice Cream recipe (see above)
3½ ounces dark chocolate (70% cocoa solids), grated

Follow the method given for vanilla ice cream, then, just before you finish churning, when the ice cream is almost firm enough to freeze, add the grated chocolate, and churn for only 2 minutes more. Freeze.

Banana Ice Cream

Serves 6

1 x Vanilla Ice Cream recipe (see above)
2 large ripe (but not brown) bananas

Follow the method given for vanilla ice cream. At the very last minute (to prevent it turning brown), dice the banana, add to the mixture in the ice cream machine, and churn a little, but do not mash the banana too much. Freeze.

Strawberry Ice Cream

Serves 6

1 x Vanilla Ice Cream recipe (see page 140)
1⅓ cups fresh strawberries
⅜ cup plus 1 tablespoon powdered sugar

Chop half the strawberries into ¼-inch pieces.

Purée the remaining strawberries with the powdered sugar and strain through a fine sieve.

Just before you finish churning the vanilla ice cream, add the strawberry pieces and churn to break them down a little more.

When you are ready to take the ice cream out of the machine, pour in the purée and churn a little to get a rippled effect. Freeze for an hour, then serve.

Pistachio Ice Cream

Serves 6

1 x Vanilla Ice Cream recipe (see page 140)
¼ cup shelled pistachio nuts

Blanch the pistachio nuts by covering them with boiling water, cooking on 100% power for one minute in the microwave, or bubbling for the same duration on top of the stove. Drain well, then slip off the skins. Finely chop the nuts and set them aside to dry on a plate.

Add the chopped pistachio nuts to the basic ice cream mixture before churning.

Honey and Cinnamon Ice Cream

Serves 6

2 cups soy milk
3 tablespoons honey
2 sticks cinnamon
6 egg yolks
¼ cup superfine sugar
⅝ cup non-dairy creamer

Heat the milk, honey, and cinnamon sticks in a pan and simmer for 5 minutes. Remove from the heat and allow to infuse for 10 minutes.

Whisk together the egg yolks and sugar until pale.

Pour the milk into the egg mixture, whisking continuously, then return to the pan and heat to 175°F, so it is pasteurized. Cool in a bowl of iced water. When cold, add the creamer and churn in an ice cream machine until firm. Freeze.

141

Sorbet Syrup

Makes 4 ½ cups

4½ cups superfine sugar
4 cups water
½ cup light corn syrup

Place the ingredients in a pan and simmer for 3 minutes. Once cool, it can be kept almost indefinitely in a sealed jar in the refrigerator or dry store until you need it.

Mango Sorbet

Serves 6

142

12 ripe (but not bruised) mangoes, peeled and pitted
¾ cup plus 1 tablespoon sorbet syrup (see above)
juice of 2 lemons

Place the mango flesh with about ½ cup of the sorbet syrup and the lemon juice in a blender, then blend until smooth. Pass through a coarse sieve.

Taste the mango purée and, if necessary, add more sorbet syrup and lemon juice—the amount will depend on the juice/acid in the mango, but bear in mind that sorbets lose a bit of sweetness on freezing.

Churn until firm in an ice cream machine, then freeze.

Raspberry Sorbet

Serves 6

8 cups raspberries
1⅔ cups sorbet syrup (see above)
juice of 1 lemon

Place the raspberries in a blender with 1¼ cups of the sorbet syrup and the lemon juice and blend until smooth. Pass through a fine sieve.

Taste the raspberry purée and, if necessary, add more syrup, bearing in mind that sorbets lose a bit of sweetness on freezing.

Churn in an ice cream machine until firm, then freeze.

Lemon Sorbet

Serves 6

zest and juice of 7 large lemons
2 cups sorbet syrup (see above)

Slowly mix the sorbet syrup with the lemon zest and juice, whisking continuously, until the balance of acidity and sweetness is about right—you will probably need about 1⅔ cups, but bear in mind that sorbets lose a bit of sweetness on freezing.

Churn in an ice cream machine until firm, then freeze.

Passion Fruit Sorbet

Serves 6

4 passion fruit
1¼ cups sorbet syrup (see opposite)
juice of a lemon

Cut the passion fruit in half, scoop out the seeds, flesh, and juice, and discard the hard skin. Mix the passion fruit with the sorbet syrup.

Taste and, if necessary, add some lemon juice, but bear in mind that sorbets lose a bit of sweetness on freezing.

Churn in an ice cream machine until firm, then freeze.

Champagne Sorbet

Serves 6

3⅓ cups champagne
1¼ cups sorbet syrup (see opposite)
juice of a lemon

Mix the Champagne and lemon juice with the sorbet syrup.

Churn in an ice cream machine until firm, then freeze.

Lime Sorbet

Serves 6

zest and juice of 10 very large firm limes
2 cups sorbet syrup (see opposite)

Gradually mix the sorbet syrup with the lime zest and juice, whisking continuously.

Churn in an ice cream machine until firm, then freeze.

❋ If you prefer a more mellow taste, you can first simmer together the syrup, juice, and zest for 5 minutes.

Pink Grapefruit Sorbet

Serves 6

143

zest and juice of 7 pink grapefruit
2 cups sorbet syrup (see opposite)

Gradually mix the sorbet syrup with the grapefruit zest and juice, whisking continuously, until you have the balance of acidity and sweetness you like, but bear in mind that sorbets lose a bit of sweetness on freezing.

Churn in an ice cream machine until firm, then freeze.

Petit Fours

Plain Tuiles

Serves 6

⅞ cup powdered sugar
3 egg whites
7 tablespoons softened margarine
¾ cup plus 1 tablespoon all-purpose flour

Preheat the oven to 425°F.

Mix together all the ingredients until smooth.

To make tuiles for petit fours, first make a circular stencil. You can do this by cutting a circle out of a plastic lid or old ice cream container, with a 2-inch circular hole in the middle of it.

Place the stencil on a nonstick baking sheet, spread the tuile mixture over it with a palette knife, then carefully lift it off, leaving behind a little round disc *(top right)*.

Repeat until the baking sheet is covered with discs.

Bake for 6 minutes or until the edges turn golden.

While still warm, lift the tuile cookies from the tray *(center right)* and lay them in a tuile tray *(bottom right)*. Alternatively, shape them over a rolling pin, if making petit fours, or over a small glass or cup if making tuile baskets.

❄ The basic mixture can be stored in the refrigerator for several days, then used for various recipes.

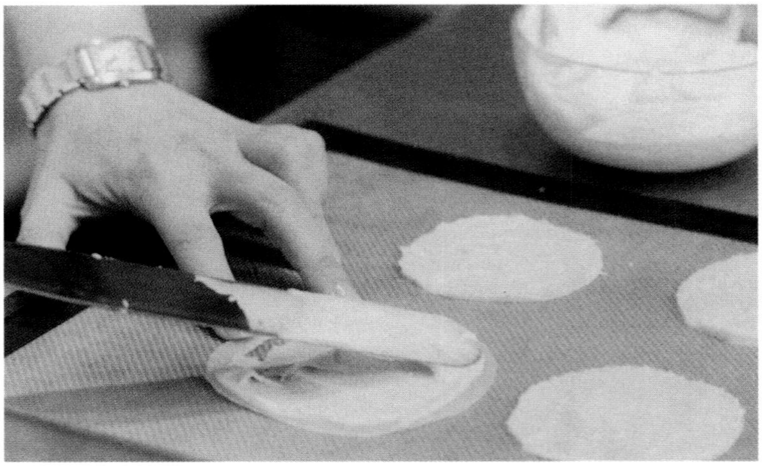

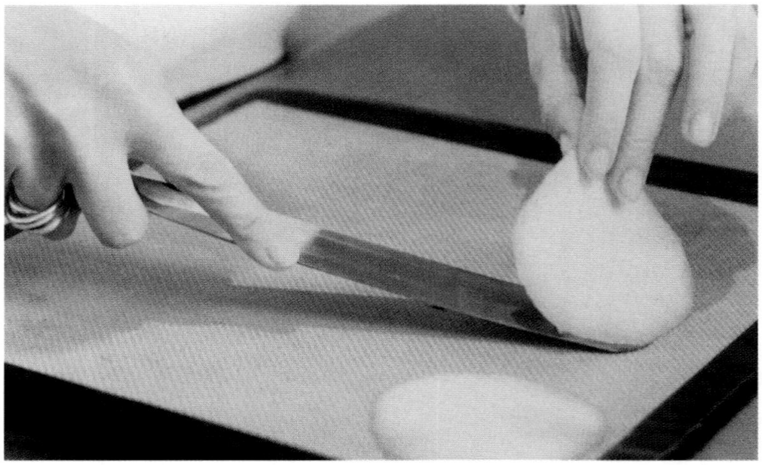

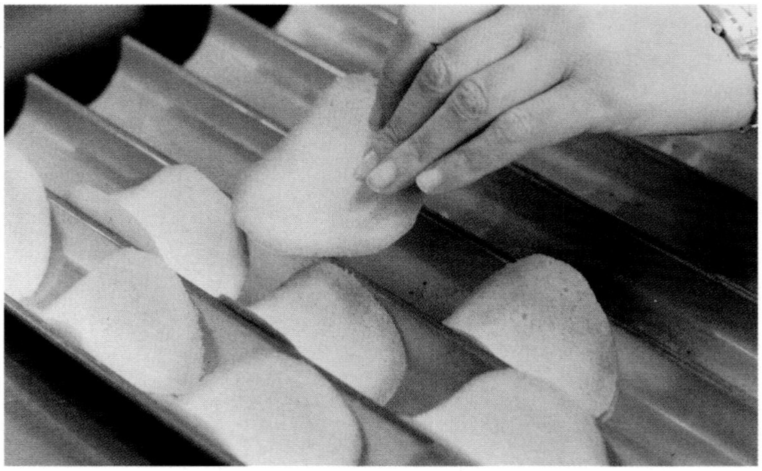

Opposite: Plain Tuiles

Chocolate Tuiles

Serves 6

7 tablespoons softened margarine

⅞ cup powdered sugar

3 egg whites

⅓ cup all-purpose flour

½ cup unsweetened cocoa powder

Follow the method on page 146.

Orange Tuiles

Serves 6

7 tablespoons softened margarine

⅞ cup powdered sugar

3 egg whites

1 cup all-purpose flour

zest of 3 oranges

¼ cup orange juice

Follow the method on page 146.

Coconut Tuiles

Serves 6

7 tablespoons softened margarine

⅞ cup powdered sugar

3 egg whites

¾ cup plus 1 tablespoon all-purpose flour

¼ cup coconut milk

1 cup toasted dried coconut

Follow the method on page 146.

❋ Chef's Tip

*Here Sobell uses a tuile tray to shape her tuiles,
but you can easily do it by shaping them
around a rolling pin or a glass.*

NEW JEWISH CUISINE

Mini Chocolate Ices on Sticks

Serves 6

1 x Vanilla Ice Cream recipe (see page 140)
10½ ounces dark chocolate (70% cocoa solids)

Ball the ice cream with a melon baller and refreeze
for an hour.

Melt the chocolate in a glass bowl set over a pan of
simmering water. (Alternatively, melt it in a Pyrex bowl in
the microwave, heating it for 10 seconds at a time, stirring
and repeating.)

Insert a cocktail stick into a ball of ice cream, dip it in
the chocolate, then refreeze.

Passion Fruit Sorbet
Dipped in Chocolate

Serves 6

1 x Passion Fruit Sorbet recipe (see page 143)
10½ ounces dark chocolate (70% cocoa solids)

Ball the passion fruit sorbet using a melon baller, then
refreeze for 3 hours.

Melt the chocolate in a glass bowl set over a pan of
simmering water. (Alternatively, melt it in a Pyrex bowl in
the microwave, heating it for 10 seconds at a time, stirring
and repeating.)

Insert a cocktail stick into a ball, dip it in the chocolate,
and refreeze until ready to serve.

Hazelnut Clusters

Serves 6

2 cups hazelnuts
1¼ cups superfine sugar

Preheat the oven to 375°F. Blanch the hazelnuts by
covering them with boiling water and bubbling for a
minute on top of the stove. Drain well, then slip off the
skins. Roast the nuts in the oven for 15 minutes until golden.

Put the sugar in a heavy-bottomed pan with ¼ cup
water and heat until it has dissolved and caramelized.

Stir the hazelnuts into the caramel and spread out on
an oiled baking tray. When cool enough to touch, take four
caramel-covered hazelnuts and shape into a pyramid.
Repeat until all hazelnuts are used.

Allow to cool completely, then store in an airtight container.

149

Cape Gooseberries
Dipped in Caramel

Serves 6

5–6 Cape gooseberries
1¼ cups superfine sugar
¼ cup water

Put the sugar in a heavy-bottomed pan with the water and
heat until the sugar has dissolved and caramelized.

Peel back the outer leaves and dip the fruits in the
caramel. Make sure you don't get caramel on your fingers
—it's hot. Leave to cool on a plate.

❋ The dipped fruit will only last 8 hours.

150

Brandy Snaps

Serves 6

9 tablespoons margarine, melted

¾ cup brown sugar

⅜ cup golden syrup

1 cup all-purpose flour

1 teaspoon brandy

1 teaspoon ground ginger

Preheat the oven to 375°F.

Place all the ingredients in a food processor and blend until smooth. Roll into small marble-sized balls, place on a baking sheet, and flatten slightly with the back of a spoon.

Bake for 8–10 minutes until they are golden brown— they will now look flat and perforated.

Allow to cool slightly, then mold over a rolling pin, if making petit fours, or over a small glass, if making baskets for ice cream.

Strawberry Tartlets

Makes 4

FOR THE PASTRY

1¾ cup all-purpose flour

¼ cup sugar

pinch of salt

10 tablespoons margarine, cut into pieces

1 egg yolk

1 tablespoon soy milk

≈

½ cup crème anglaise (see page 118)

¾ cup strawberries, thinly sliced

Make the pastry by putting the flour, margarine, salt, and sugar into a food processor, then pulse until it resembles breadcrumbs. Add the egg and milk and pulse once more until a dough has formed. Wrap in plastic wrap and allow to rest for 2 hours.

Preheat the oven to 425°F. Roll out the pastry on a lightly-floured surface and use to line four 1½-inch tartlet cases. Bake blind for 20 minutes (see Chef's Tip).

Just before serving— and no more than 4 hours beforehand—fill the pastry cases with the crème anglaise and top with the strawberries.

151

✳ Chef's Tip

Baking blind means cooking the pastry on its own. Put the pastry in a lightly-greased dish according to recipe. Line the pastry case with parchment paper, weight it with baking beans or dried raw pulses, and bake until three-quarters done, or according to recipe.

Opposite, clockwise from left: Truffles, Cape Gooseberry Dipped in Caramel, Tuiles, Brandy Snap, Hazelnut Cluster, Strawberry Tartlet

Palmiers

Serves 20

8½ ounces puff pastry
⅞ ounces powdered sugar
1 teaspoon cinnamon

Roll out the pastry on a lightly-floured surface to a thickness of about ⅛ inch, and roughly 14 inches square.

Dust with the powdered sugar and cinnamon, then roll up like a Swiss roll and chill for an hour.

Preheat the oven to 450°F.

Trim the ends of the roll, slice into discs ⅛ inch thick, place them flat on a greased baking tray, and bake for 6–10 minutes.

Dust with powdered sugar before serving. Eat the same day they are cooked.

Honey Madeleines

Serves 20

Deliciously sweet, soft-textured petit fours for when you really want an impressive finish to a special occasion meal. You could even serve them at a cocktail party as a sweet appetizer. Easy to make, they also store well in an airtight container for up to three days.

2 eggs
⅜ cup sugar
2 teaspoons brown sugar
⅜ cup plus 2 tablespoons
  all-purpose flour
1 teaspoon baking powder
6 tablespoons margarine,
  melted
1 teaspoon honey

❖ Chef's Tip

For a soft-centered surprise, place a raspberry in the center of each mold before baking.

You will need a madeleine tray for this recipe—you can buy one at any specialty kitchenware store.

Beat the egg and sugars together until pale in color.

Sift together the flour and baking powder, and fold into the egg mixture.

Stir in the melted margarine and honey, then allow to rest in the refrigerator for an hour.

Preheat the oven to 450°F.

Lightly grease a madeleine tray, then dust with flour. Spoon in the mixture and bake for 5 minutes.

Leave to cool.

Chocolate Truffles

Serves 6

10½ ounces chocolate (70% cocoa solids)
11 tablespoons margarine, melted
½ cup non-dairy creamer
3 tablespoons alcohol, such as brandy, rum, or
crème de menthe
cocoa powder for dusting
powdered sugar for dusting

Melt the chocolate in a glass bowl set over a pan of simmering water. (Alternatively, melt it in a Pyrex bowl in the microwave, heating it for 10 seconds at a time, stirring and repeating.)

Whisk the creamer into the melted margarine, add the alcohol, then whisk into the melted chocolate.

Chill. When set, shape into balls using a small melon baller. Roll in cocoa powder then dust with powdered sugar, and refrigerate until ready to serve.

Coconut Truffles

Serves 6

10½ ounces chocolate (70% cocoa solids)
½ cup coconut milk
11 tablespoons margarine, melted
3 tablespoons coconut rum liqueur such as Malibu
¾ cup dried coconut

Melt the chocolate in a glass bowl set over a pan of simmering water. (Alternatively, melt it in a Pyrex bowl in the microwave, heating it for 10 seconds at a time, stirring and repeating.)

Melt the margarine in a pan or in the microwave. Whisk in the coconut milk, add the Malibu, then whisk this into the melted chocolate. Chill in the refrigerator.

Lightly toast the coconut on a baking sheet under a hot broiler for a few seconds.

When the truffle mixture is set, shape it into balls using a small melon baller, and roll them in dried coconut.

Refrigerate until ready to serve.

153

Orange Truffles

Serves 6

1 pound 2 ounces dark chocolate (70% cocoa solids)
½ cup non-dairy creamer
11 tablespoons margarine, melted
3 tablespoons Grand Marnier
zest of 2 oranges

Melt 10½ ounces of the chocolate in a glass bowl set over a pan of simmering water. (Alternatively, melt it in a Pyrex bowl in the microwave, heating it for 10 seconds at a time, stirring and repeating.) Melt the remaining chocolate in a separate bowl.

Melt the margarine in a pan or in the microwave. Whisk in the creamer, add the Grand Marnier and orange zest, then whisk the creamer mixture into the larger amount of melted chocolate. Chill in the refrigerator.

When cold, shape into balls using a small melon baller, dip in the second bowl of melted chocolate, and refrigerate until ready to serve.

Hazelnut Truffles

Serves 6

10½ ounces dark chocolate (70% cocoa solids)
½ cup non-dairy creamer
11 tablespoons margarine, melted
3 tablespoons rum
2 cups hazelnuts, finely chopped

Melt the chocolate in a glass bowl set over a pan of simmering water. (Alternatively, melt it in a Pyrex bowl in the microwave, heating it for 10 seconds at a time, stirring and repeating.)

Melt the margarine in a pan or in the microwave. Whisk in the creamer, add the rum and half the hazelnuts, then whisk into the melted chocolate. Chill in the refrigerator.

When cold, shape into balls using a small melon baller, roll them in the remaining hazelnuts, and refrigerate until ready to serve.

154

Opposite: Assorted truffles

Entertaining

Eating in has become one of the great "nights out,"

whether it's with family and friends for a special occasion

or just as a way of relaxing at home.

The formal dinner party has given way to a

more casual style of entertaining at home, but

getting it right still depends on careful planning....

A feast for the eyes

First impressions count for a lot—and that's as true of food as it is of people. Get the look right and you're halfway to creating a culinary sensation. In this chapter we take a look at a number of different scenarios for entertaining at home, with a suggested menu for each party, along with some tips for ensuring that you create the right atmosphere as well as meal to remember. The recipes are all taken from this book, and you're bound to find many other dishes that work equally well together. Just choose the combination to suit the occasion and your tastes, and enjoy putting together something special for your family and friends.

Today, whether you're throwing a dinner party for a few friends or inviting the mob over for Sunday lunch, there's a vast array of cuisines and recipes you could offer them. But while food fashions may come and go—traditional salmon is replaced with seared tuna, while black forest cake gives way to chocolate tart—the basic ingredients of successful entertaining remain the same.

It is often taken for granted that the food will be good at a catered occasion, but it's setting the scene, creating the right mood, and paying attention to detail, that turns the occasion into something memorable…and it's exactly the same if you're entertaining at home.

Here are a few guidelines to help you plan your home entertaining. Combined with a selection of tried and tested recipes from the pages of *New Jewish Cuisine*, it will help ensure that the hosts enjoy their evening as much as their guests!

The guests

Food has always been at the heart of a Jewish home, from the traditional Friday night dinner to special festivals for family and relatives. But entertaining at home is no longer just for these occasions—it's also an opportunity to bring together friends, from a wider circle, with differing tastes and cultural influences.

It is important to consider the mix of people and what sort of conversation and atmosphere you are likely to get when you add them together! You should also think about how many you can comfortably accommodate, depending on the occasion. For example, around six to eight o'clock should be right for a dinner party where you want to keep everyone involved in the conversation. If it's cocktail hour before going out, you may like to invite many more—but if that means standing room only, take care not to let it go on too long.

Make sure all your guests

· Menu ·

Tartar of Smoked Salmon

RECIPE ON PAGE 51

Roast Rack of Lamb with Pommes Anna

RECIPE ON PAGE 109

Chocolate Truffle Heart with Summer Berry Fruits and Raspberry Coulis

RECIPE ON PAGE 118

≈

The Romantic Dinner for Two

159

Scene-setting is essential if you're planning a romantic rendezvous for two, but you also want to spend your time with your partner, and not in the kitchen. So greet your special someone with well-chilled champagne, enjoy a delicious dinner that you've prepared in advance, finish with an irresistible dessert—and leave the dishes until the morning! Much of the work for this menu can be done in advance, so once you've dressed the table you'll have lots of time to dress for dinner. It offers a delicious salmon starter, ready to serve at the table before sitting down, and an impressive main course. Vegetables can be blanched earlier in the evening, then simply refreshed in hot water before serving. The lamb can be prepared and sealed ready to pop into a hot oven. To keep the romantic theme, the rack of lamb can be cut in half and arranged in a heart shape on the plate. And it's all rounded off—of course—with a chocolate heart.

know who else has been invited and try to give them a few background details such as shared interests to help break the ice. Give them an idea of what to expect—whether it's going to be snacks with drinks, a light supper, or a full three-course dinner.

It's important to make an effort to meet individual tastes and diets. Do all your guests keep kosher? Is anyone allergic to nuts? Any vegetarians? Or does some awkward soul simply hate a particular ingredient?

If your invitation includes children, make sure you have catered for their needs and tastes too. If you have young children of your own but it's adult-only time you're after, then make sure they have their own entertainment sorted out—or that you've allowed plenty of time for them to be safely tucked into bed before your guests arrive.

Once you've got your guest list sorted out, better start getting ready for the show…

Some dishes definitely need to be prepared in advance!
Try your hand at this spectacular dessert on page 128.

It may be tempting to offer the same old favorites so you don't have the worry of offering your guests something you've never cooked before. But what a shame to miss out on an opportunity to surprise your family and friends with something new and interesting, particularly if it's a special occasion. So, once you've chosen your dishes, practice them first. Then look at how much you could prepare in advance and freeze, chill, or store until the big event.

Finally, plan to have a back-up ready for that precisely timed hot soufflé at which someone just could not resist taking a peek! A refreshing fruit salad and good ice cream, nicely presented, is easy to prepare in advance and will still provide a perfect finish to your meal.

Much of the table presentation can also be done in advance—here are a few suggestions to add to your dinner party checklist:

❇ Make sure you have matching polished silverware and glassware

❇ Hand-polish plates—to avoid fingerprints, make sure your hands are not wet when handling the edges

❇ Choose coordinating, well-pressed table linens

❇ A cold appetizer can already by set on the table

❇ For a special party, sprinkle glitter on the tablecloth for added sparkle

❇ Dessert plates can be decorated in advance if you have enough room to lay them out

Preparation

Good planning will take a lot of the hard work out of entertaining at home—and it should leave stress-free hosts able to enjoy the meal with their guests.

Give yourself plenty of time to plan your menu and work out a schedule for the evening to make sure all your dishes come together at the right time, to avoid a last-minute panic.

The Traditional Sunday Dinner

· Menu ·

Cream of Vegetable Soup
with Garlic Croûtons

OR

Crown of Melon with a
Cascade of Berry Fruits

RECIPES ON PAGES 37 AND 42

Traditional Roast Beef
with Yorkshire Pudding
and Seasonal Vegetables

RECIPE ON PAGE 115

Apple and Blackberry Crumble
with Raspberry Coulis and
Crème Anglaise and
Vanilla Ice Cream
in a Tuile Basket

RECIPE ON PAGE 136

≈

Few people can resist an invitation to Sunday dinner, but if the host is to enjoy the day as much as the guests, the first rule is: Start early! This menu, with a choice of starters and desserts, should suit most families. Much can be prepared in advance—the soup can be frozen—but don't make fruit salad before the day, and pep it up with fresh orange juice just before serving. The individual crumbles can be made as one large dessert, if you prefer. When it comes to roast beef, I find the best kosher cut often is the ball of the rib—a little expensive but well worth it. Ask your butcher for a piece that's well-hung, so it's tender. Don't skimp on the roast—allow a 4–5 pound piece for a family of six. Any leftovers can always be served as cold cuts the next day, though its doubtful you'll have much left!

Scene-setting

Giving some thought to the kind of atmosphere you want to create for your guests will really enhance the occasion. Think about the style of food you have chosen to serve and how you would like it to look on the plate and at the table —then create an appropriate setting with your choice of tableware and decorations, lighting, and music. Don't forget, the food is only half the occasion; the scene you set will transform a meal into a memorable event.

Here are a few scene-setting tips to remember:
✳ Organize some cool background music, but not too loud
✳ Dress the table with flowers, candles, or garden foliage
✳ Plan the lighting to ensure a warm atmosphere—candles add a soft glow to a dinner party and should be lit before guests are seated at the table. Scented candles can add to the atmosphere, but make sure they are not too strong or they'll be overpowering
✳ For more formal events, use name cards at each setting. Try something eye-catching and unusual—a gold pen to write on a leaf from the garden, for example
✳ Serve coffee in the living room if possible to allow your guests to relax away from the dining table

Bring on the food!

It doesn't matter whether it's a lavish dinner or a simple bowl of salad, when it comes to serving your food, presentation is the key. Set out to impress—and satisfy your guests by feeding their eyes first.

Here's how to make your meal a real show-stopper:
✳ Use large presentation dishes that will display your food at its best
✳ Depending on the dish, dust the plate with paprika, powdered sugar, or cocoa powder
✳ To add color and dimension, garnish the plate with fresh herbs, or use a banana leaf on the base of the plate and serve the food on top

✳ Don't be tempted to pile too much on the plate. Instead, carefully place potatoes and vegetables around meat or fish to really enhance the presentation
✳ For an imaginative way to serve appetizers, cover pieces of wood with remnants of material or use slate tiles or even spare floor tiles that have been varnished
✳ If you're serving nibbles with drinks, make sure they are easy-to-handle bite-size pieces
✳ Always have white wine very well chilled and serve it in sparkling clean and polished glasses
✳ Make sure you have still and/or sparkling water to offer. Add a twist of lime or lemon to water glasses and if you have no room to chill the water, then add ice cubes to the glasses. Look for bottled water in an attractive colored container that would match your table décor

Finally, remember that, whatever you serve to your guests, aim to feast their eyes first so that they will enjoy the meal from the first glimpse to the last mouthful. Appetizers and desserts provide great opportunities to really surprise and delight people with a particularly delicious little treat.

That attention to detail and the desire to serve beautiful food have strongly influenced the recipes offered in this book. I hope you find them as much fun as I do!

Carole Sobell's

· Menu ·

Smoked Salmon Rosettes

RECIPE ON PAGE 18

Fish and Chips

RECIPE ON PAGE 26

Thai Chicken Satay

RECIPE ON PAGE 25

Mini Potato Latkes

RECIPE ON PAGE 31

Thai Fish Cakes

RECIPE ON PAGE 29

Petit Fours

VARIOUS RECIPES ON PAGES 146–154

Cape Gooseberries in Caramel

RECIPE ON PAGE 149

Dark chocolate mints

≈

The Drinks Party

If you're catering for a crowd, or simply want to relax with friends, then appetizers are the answer. It's a favorite way of entertaining because you can create some fabulous treats and they look great. But it shouldn't mean that anyone goes home hungry! Start with cold appetizers, so you have something to offer people right away. Smoked salmon is a good appetizer to get the taste buds ready for a variety of cold and hot treats. Use your imagination to think of fresh ways to serve your appetizers. Brighten up the tray with a few flowers or leaves, a candle, or a handful of berries. When the party includes children, it's fun to serve appetizers that are miniature favorite meals like burgers and french fries in paper cones. End with a selection of petit fours—any dessert in the book can be served in mini form—and then serve mints with coffee.

The Celebration Dinner

There are times when you want to make an extra effort to mark an important anniversary, a family gathering, or other special occasion—and what better way than to treat your guests to a fine dinner?

Make sure you can offer something special to everyone, including a choice of dishes to tempt all tastes and preferences, perhaps a fish dish or an interesting vegetarian course. Prepare as much as possible in advance so that you too can join in the celebrations. In the menu shown here, even the potato rosti can be made ahead of time then reheated to a hot and perfectly crisp dish at the last moment. For the noisettes of lamb, allow a generous four slices per person—you should get about one-and-a-half portions per loin of lamb. When it comes to finishing a special occasion meal, it has to be a soufflé—it's a spectacular dessert that is

164

· Menu ·

Wild Mushroom Soup

RECIPE ON PAGE 36

Noisettes of Lamb with Potato and Parsnip Rosti
AND **a Panache of Vegetables**

RECIPES ON PAGES 106 AND 107

Individual Chocolate Soufflés

TOPPED WITH BERRIES AND

Crème Anglaise

RECIPES ON PAGES 132 AND 136

≈

bound to impress, and it's not as difficult as you might imagine once you're not afraid of it. You should, however, practice making a soufflé before serving it at an important celebration—but as long as your soufflé rises to the occasion, so will you!

✳ Style Tip
*Candles bring a glow
to any dinner table—even
if you don't
have an elaborate
candelabra like this
exotic arrangement!*

165

Index

166

167

❋ Final Tip

*Enjoy yourself,
and the food!*